THE LAST FREEDOM

The Last Freedom

Mary Craig

Hodder & Stoughton

LONDON SYDNEY AUCKLAND

British Library Cataloguing in Publication Data
A record for this book is available from the British Library

ISBN 0 340 69079 8

Typeset by Avon Dataset Ltd, Bidford-on-Avon, Warks

Printed and bound in Great Britain by
Mackays of Chatham PLC, Chatham, Kent

Hodder and Stoughton Ltd
A division of Hodder Headline PLC
338 Euston Road
London NW1 3BH

For Maureen and Peter,
Sue, Desmond, Anne, Mike, Margaret and Joe
with gratitude and love

Everything can be taken from a man but one thing: the last of the human freedoms – to choose one's attitude in any given set of circumstances, to choose one's own way . . .

Viktor Frankl, *Man's Search for Meaning*

The facts of life and death are neutral. We, by our responses, give suffering either a positive or a negative meaning. Illnesses, accidents, human tragedies kill people. But they do not necessarily kill life or faith. If the death and suffering of someone we love makes us bitter, jealous, against all religion, and incapable of happiness, *we* turn the person who died into one of the 'devil's martyrs.' If suffering and death in someone close to us bring us to explore the limits of our capacity for strength and love and cheerfulness, if it leads us to discover sources of consolation we never knew before, then *we* make the person into a witness for the affirmation of life rather than its rejection.

Rabbi Harold S. Kushner, *When Bad Things Happen to Good People*

THANK YOU

To the doctors and nurses at Woolton Hill surgery and to Madeleine, our Macmillan nurse, for their more than kindness.

To Professor Raoul Coombes for his tireless efforts on Frank's behalf.

To Margaret Griffiths and Frances Donnelly for encouraging me to have this journal published.

And to all the friends who in their many different ways helped to see me through a painful period of my life.

INTRODUCTION

I met Frank towards the end of my first term in Oxford, shortly after the end of the Second World War. The country was still plagued by austerity and rationing, but there was hope too and relief that the fighting was over at last and the ex-servicemen were coming home. For us it was a happy time. We got engaged even before we graduated and married three years later in 1952. Our marriage produced four sons, two of whom, alas, were mentally handicapped. The presence of Paul and Nicholas in our family might have destroyed us, but though life was always difficult and at times our marriage came under strain, Frank and I accepted the situation and were determined to survive it.

I suppose that, like many other couples, we muddled along somehow, sometimes satisfactorily, sometimes not. As the children grew older, there were crisis moments when each of us in turn considered leaving, but somehow we could never quite bring ourselves to that point. The fact was, we were always each other's best friend.

After Frank retired, in 1987, he concentrated on looking after our large garden and on voluntary work for various charities connected with mental handicap. By the time we entered this new phase of our lives, I had for some years been a fairly successful writer and had produced, apart from the better-known *Blessings* and *Man from a Far Country*, several biographies and contemporary histories. I was then just about to begin work on a book about the Tibetan refugees in India. Our first handicapped son, Paul, had died in 1966 at the age of ten. Anthony, our eldest, was a successful computer analyst. Mark, a veterinary surgeon, was soon to marry Trish Sugden, a fellow vet. Nick, our 23-year-old Down's syndrome youngest son, still lived with us and was the pride and joy of the whole family. It's fair to say that he was the light of Frank's life, and indeed none of us could have borne to think of life without him.

Two years later, in the autumn of 1990, Frank and I went through another of our crises, but this one, oddly enough, led to perhaps the happiest period of our entire life together. We had no idea that time was running out on us. Though the reality was that cancer was already present in his right lung, everybody was remarking that Frank looked fitter and happier than ever before. It was an illusion. In July 1994 it became apparent that, unbelievable though it might be, he had little time to live. The news was devastating. For all of us it came as the kind of seismic shock which irrevocably alters the shape of one's entire existence.

Whenever life has threatened to overwhelm me, I have always instinctively reached for pen and paper to keep some sort of record. This time was no different. I needed to try to make sense of the pain, hurt, fear and sheer bewilderment that had crowded in on me since the discovery of Frank's illness. This wouldn't – and didn't – prevent me being furious at fate for putting a time-bomb under my life just when I had begun to feel that things were going well for us. But trying to give meaning to the experience helped. The journal, written for the most part when Frank was asleep, became crucial to my survival.

For the eight months that remained to us, Frank became the sole focus of my life as together we faced his approaching death. Anyone who has lived with a terminally ill loved one throughout the last months of his or her life, will have experienced that strange state of semi-suspension in which everyday life seems less substantial than the vigil one keeps at the dying person's bedside. Yet into this enforced sojourn in no-man's-land an unlooked-for comfort comes. Half-remembered snatches of poetry, paragraphs from well-loved books, suddenly surface bringing with them shafts of illumination and a promise, still shadowy and undefined perhaps, that somewhere there is healing to be found. This, together with the unfailing support of friends, the under-standing letters we received, and the care shown us by doctors and nurses all contributed towards making the unbearable more bearable.

As I went on adding to this journal, it gradually metamor-phosed into an anthology and also into a sounding-box where I could let off steam. It provided, in fact, the best kind of therapy. I didn't reread what I had written – I simply didn't want to – but as Frank's death approached, the journal became the repository for all the anguish which I couldn't show him.

Yet, when I finished writing it, on the Easter Sunday after his death, I just put it into a cupboard in my study and forgot about it. It was not until over a year later, when one of my oldest friends, Margaret Griffiths (our friendship dates from kindergarten days, when we were both four) was staying with me, that I recalled the journal and told her about it. Margaret asked if she could see it, and with some misgivings I took it from the cupboard and handed it to her. When she had finished reading, she came downstairs in tears. 'I don't know if you have any plans for this,' she said, 'but I really think it ought to be published. It could help a lot of people. It's already helped *me*.'

After Margaret had gone, I made myself read the journal through for the first time. I wept, of course, as I was pitched back into that traumatic time with all its attendant pain and grief. At the same time I could recognise that all those fragments of other people's wisdom, clawed desperately out of the air at the time, *had* helped me towards an insight into what was happening. Perhaps Margaret was right; if there *had* been some kind of illumination, it ought to be shared. But I couldn't quite face the idea of publication. Not yet. The journal was too private.

On the other hand, there was the example of *Blessings*; that had been private too. In *Blessings* I had felt impelled to try and interpret another experience that had marked me and changed my life for ever. And in exploring the nature of my own suffering, I seem to have touched a universal nerve. Hundreds of men and women all over the world responded to the book as though it was *their* pain that was being addressed, and as though for the first time they were being shown a way of coming to terms with it. For over two years after the book came out – in 1979 – I spent the best part of every morning answering letters. Seventeen years later, the letters are still coming in, though less frequently now, since the book has been temporarily out of print.

Over the years, many people, including various publishers, had suggested I should write a sequel. But I always knew that a sequel, in the sense in which they probably envisaged it, was out of the question. *Blessings* had never been intended as autobiography; it was a reflective piece, born of a painful period in my life, such as I hoped never to go through again. Only another personal catastrophe could bring forth a sequel – and I fervently hoped that this would never happen. I was keeping my head well down, hoping that the fates had done with me and would leave me alone.

Suddenly I realised that the sequel to *Blessings* had perhaps already been written. I decided to wait and see what happened. Six months later, Hodder decided to update and re-issue *Blessings*. Judith Longman, an editorial director with the company, came to see me to discuss plans. On impulse, as I went to the kitchen to get the lunch, I showed her the journal, without explanation, and left her to leaf through it. By the time I returned to say that lunch was ready, she had decided she wanted to publish it. The matter seemed to have been taken out of my hands: the journal would be the sequel to *Blessings*. There could be no other.

If there is a common theme shared by these two books, it is that we humans have to be forcibly parted from our old selves before we will acknowledge unavoidable change. We believe that only worldly success defines our progress through life. Yet my own experience has taught me that the concepts of success and failure become irrelevant when the struggle is simply to survive. My friend, Donald Nicholl, has written that the essence of suffering lies in the fact that initiative is taken out of our own hands:

> So long as our lives are in our own hands we will never really give up the very thing we need above all to give up if we are to be changed, whether that thing is our money, our house, our good name, our health or our very life. What we do not want to give up is precisely the thing that it is necessary for us to give up if we are to grow. And we would never do so unless we were thrust into it of necessity.[1]

Though sadly, when the immediate crisis is over, we tend to lose sight of even the most painfully won insights, I have found that one central discovery has stayed with me from both these periods of my life: that at the moment of greatest desolation we become aware that strength is available for us if we choose to avail ourselves of it. Seizing hold of that strength, choosing to face an uncertain future with hope rather than immerse oneself in the wreckage of one's past, is the one important freedom we have. Ultimately, if we are to grow as human beings, it is not the external circumstances of our lives which shape us, but how we choose to respond to them.

It is not easy to find the right words to communicate what seems to me to be a profound and universal truth about life. As Flaubert tell us so memorably, 'Human language is like a cracked kettle on which we beat out tunes for bears to dance to, when all the time we long to move the stars to pity.' Words tend to fail us when most we need them. But I believe it is important to try, and, however inadequate words may be, they are the only tools I have.

Mary Craig
December 1996

Friday 25 January 1991

Suddenly I'm scared. Fate seems to have a bizarre sense of humour, to say nothing of timing. Just as we had got things sorted out between us and the future looked promising, we're told that Frank may have lung cancer. It's only a possibility – the merest hint of a shadow on an X-ray picture – and we shan't know anything more till next week after he's had a bronchoscopy. But fear has already taken root.

Friday 1 February 1991

Two days ago, following the biopsy done at Battle Hospital I went with Frank to see Mr L, the lung specialist. I didn't want him to have to go alone. Mr L told Frank there was no sign of a tumour, and later that afternoon Johnny Vooght (a doctor friend and neighbour) convinced us that cancer was most unlikely since everybody has been commenting on how fit and well Frank suddenly looks, and how we both seem so much happier. We were considerably cheered. So today – when we went to see Mr L for the second time and he spoke of more tests to be done, more tissues to be analysed – it came as a shock. He told us he had a gut feeling that some cells will turn out to be cancerous – though, if they do, he assured us they can be cured by surgery. So is it good news or bad? Where do we go from here? We came away confused and disoriented. Life has suddenly taken on different parameters, and we don't know where we are.

Saturday 2 February 1991

We should have been going to Johnny and Mary's golden

wedding party tomorrow, but we don't feel very sociable. Nick has gone to Poynings (the hostel attached to his day centre) for a week, so we're taking the opportunity to go to Bournemouth for a long week-end instead – lots of walks along the cliff-tops and plenty of fresh air. Actually we're not unhopeful. Everyone seems convinced that if Mr L says a cure will be possible, then it must be possible – he wouldn't promise such a thing lightly. Clutching at straws, of course, but straws are there to be clutched at.

Came across these words by Carlo Carretto, in a little book I once wrote the Introduction to:

> For this is precisely our tragedy: we think we know when in fact we know nothing; we think we can see when in fact we are blind. What do we know of death, of eternity, of the purpose of things, of suffering, of what was before us, of what will be after us? We imagine we have a plan, when in fact we have not; we believe we know what is good for us, when all the time we may be working to destroy it . . . We are afraid of the new and mysterious. If it were left in our hands, we would ask God to stay here on our level, when all the while our happiness depends on our moving upwards towards him . . . What we lack is a true perspective, and this distorts the whole picture of our lives.[2]

But how to find that true perspective? That's the sixty-four thousand dollar question.

Friday 8 February 1991

It's been snowing heavily, and the whole country seems to have been thrown off course. I'm furious because Mr L's secretary has rung to postpone this afternoon's appointment for a week – because of the weather! How can they do this to us? Don't they understand that to a man waiting to discover if he does or doesn't have cancer, every day seems like an eternity? We're both on a knife-edge already, and the world around us seems to echo our desolation: there's the Gulf War, saturation bombing, threats of chemical warfare, troops being injected against bubonic plague, a mortar attack on the PM and Cabinet which narrowly missed killing them. There's not much to be cheerful about.

Saturday 16 February 1991

Those damned cells *were* cancerous and Mr L has referred us to a highly reputed surgeon in Wimpole Street with the reassuring name of Tom Treasure. When we went to see him today, Mr Treasure said he was 90 per cent sure Frank had lung cancer, and advised the removal of a section of the right lung. Unfortunately, he was less encouraging than we might have hoped about the chances of survival. 'Better than evens in your case,' he cautiously described the odds – a far cry from Mr L's talk of 'total cure'. We were shaken, and our steps were considerably less jaunty as we walked towards the Underground. But at least no time is being lost. The date has already been set for the operation – 4 March, two weeks from now, at St Anthony's, Cheam.

I've been reading Sheila Cassidy's *Good Friday People*. It suits my mood and helps put the situation in some kind of perspective. I feel an affinity for that friend of hers whose poem she quotes:

> We, without a future,
> Safe, defined, delivered

> Now salute you, God,
> Knowing that nothing is safe,
> Secure, inviolable here.
> Except you.[3]

Such an admission goes against the modern Western ethos. Though we are, most of us, aware that our world is flawed, since wherever we look we see evidence of 'that discord in the pact of things', we have nevertheless come to believe in our own built-in right to happiness. I remember once being interviewed on Georgetown University's campus radio in Washington, when I was promoting *Blessings* and *Man from a Far Country* on radio and TV in various parts of the United States. Afterwards I sat talking to the interviewer about some of the issues that he'd raised. 'The curse of our age,' he said with feeling, 'is our belief that we have a right not only to the *pursuit* of happiness but to happiness itself. There couldn't be a more dangerous delusion, and one day it will destroy us.' I've often thought about his words. Today in the West we are obsessed by 'rights', both real and imaginary, and are paying the price in terms of our own peace of mind. We cling to what we believe is (or should be) rightfully ours and are terrified of losing (or not acquiring) it. When we fail, we rarely look inwards and blame ourselves, but look around for convenient scapegoats. We rush to the courts at the drop of a hat, and seem to believe that everything in the world comes labelled with a price-tag. What a lot of whingers we have become!

Inner peace, I believe, comes from accepting that we have to live our lives according to – and within the considerable limitations of – the raw material which we have been given; that we don't call all the shots, however much we like to think we're in command of our destinies. We think we are entitled to the continuation of a certain cosy framework to life: this man (or woman or child), these friends, this house, my good health, my job, my reputation. And as long as we are muddling along safely in our ruts, we delude ourselves that we are in full control of our lives, ignoring the reality that we are an integral part of a constantly changing world which has not only been shaped by the good or bad actions of countless generations of human beings but which is also at the mercy of randomness. The material universe has its own freedom. There is nothing fixed within it, nothing on which we can ultimately depend. The only certainty is that everything is in flux, everything changes. Our 'control' is a mirage.

Acknowledging that change is part of what we are, Sheila Cassidy talks of a 'call to powerlessness'. We are all, she says, 'sooner or later, required to let go of the strings with which we manipulate our lives and be led "where we would rather not go".' We need to keep that in mind. 'There is a time for growth and a time for diminishment in the lives of each one of us.' wrote Teilhard. 'At one moment the dominant note is one of constructive human effort, and at another mystical annihilation.'[4]

Friday 17 May 1991

It has been an eventful and worrying few weeks. On 3 March we went to stay with Frank's twin sister, Maureen, and her husband, Peter, in Merton Park, which is no more than a short distance from St Anthony's, the hospital in Cheam where Frank was to have the operation next day.

It was a very anxious period, but it seems – what a lot of hope is invested in that word 'seems' – to have ended reasonably well. On the afternoon of 4 March when Frank was having one-third of his right lung removed at St

Anthony's, I sat at my word processor and forced myself to concentrate on an article on suffering which I had to write for a Lent series for the *Tablet*. Needless to say, I wrote it from the heart. The effort became a kind of desperate prayer, with the greater part of my mind constantly on what was being done a few miles away, in the theatre at St Anthony's. Frank telephoned me shortly after he came round from the anaesthetic, and he sounded very woozy and ill, but at least he had come through the ordeal safely. In the days that followed he made such an amazing recovery that the nurses called him 'the miracle man'. It was unbelievable.

He came back to Maureen's a week later and we then had the cliff-hanging wait for the pathology report. Anxiety sent our nerves ragged, and when Mr Treasure finally rang me with the findings, I was shaking so much I could hardly hold the phone. But then came a surge of overwhelming relief when he told me he had cut out all the cancerous tissue, there were no secondaries and apparently no cancer in the bloodstream. A few lymph glands which had been infected had been taken away. He could only hope that they'd all been caught, that there were no rogue ones that might have escaped into the bloodstream. Amen to that.

The immediate scare over, and with Frank seemingly racing back to normal at full speed, we allowed ourselves to relax. We spent a few days more with Maureen and Peter and then returned home to pick up the threads of normal living. 'You may have a year or two now,' commented my friend, Mia Woodruff, 'so make the most of your time.' Though Mia in her wisdom was gently warning that I should not take too much for granted, I was a bit sore at the implication that Frank was henceforth living on borrowed time. How rapidly the sense of danger departs once the all-clear sounds! We scurry back to our fools' paradises and bolt the door against the nasty reality outside.

Frank's health continued to improve, though, after the first few weeks, no longer in such dramatic leaps and bounds. We booked for a long convalescent week-end in Jersey, and revelled in the sunshine and good food. Everything, we were sure, was going to be fine. But following an unwise indulgence in a fry-up at the airport on the way back home, Frank began vomiting, and I was afraid the retching would damage him. To our horror, a couple of days later he began coughing up sputum again. Not blood, it's true, but since this was the very symptom that had sent him off to the doctor in the first place (in July 1990) it was enough to set the alarm bells ringing again. Next, his voice suddenly went very hoarse. Though the latest X-rays were clear, Mr L was taking no chances and arranged an appointment with an ear, nose and throat consultant in Reading. The latter discovered the right vocal chord to be partially paralysed, and Frank was booked in for another scan.

As I write this, he is having the scan at the Royal Berks Hospital. We *are* very worried, there's no denying it. The future again seems in doubt, and the uncertainty frightens me. Mary O'Hara has just given me a new version of 'Be still and know that I am God' – 'Relax and give me a chance to show you that I am God.' She seems to collect phrases like that. I try it out, but faith seems to have flown the coop and I refuse to be comforted. Yet I tell myself that if the worst happens, one will find strength somehow – 'from somewhere beyond time', as I think Simone Weil puts it. It is amazing how that is always true. It's important to grasp that, *now*, at this moment, when I am still only in the hinterland of despair.

I turn back the pages of this diary and see again the Carretto words – 'We are afraid of the new and mysterious.' Yes, I am; we are. We want to hang on to our rediscovered happiness, we want life on our terms. We want to stay as we are – or recently were – with what Merton called our 'habitual, half-tied vision of things', unwilling to risk going beyond 'the shadow and the disguise'. Suddenly I remember the Russian Orthodox Archbishop Anthony Bloom saying, 'The sick man who prays only for a cure has not learned the meaning of hope.' I was impressed by those words from the moment I heard them and I thought I'd absorbed the truth of them. But now I know I have not. I *do*, absolutely unequivocally, hope for a cure. I want out of all this.

The scan revealed nothing ominous and we breathed again. Life resumed its normal course, give or take a few hiccups like the fact that I had to have my gall-bladder removed later that month. Laser surgery being one of the miracles of modern science, I recovered in a matter of days and had soon forgotten about it. In fact, I went to India in September, to do further research for my book on Tibetan refugees. The major worry – the fear of recurring cancer – receded into the background. The regular X-rays, at first every three months, then every six, were reassuring. If Frank could go for five years like this we'd be home and dry.

Since his retirement in 1987, Frank had devoted much energy to working for Mencap, first of all as a financial adviser and troubleshooter at their London HQ, and then as vice-chairman of the local Newbury organisation. In the years following his lung operation, he battled for, found premises for, equipped, stocked, staffed and opened a second-hand shop for Mencap. Since at first nobody else shared his conviction that what Mencap needed was a charity shop, he put up the capital himself and applied all his energies to getting the project off the ground. Being the father of two mentally handicapped sons, he had always wanted to make some positive contribution like this, out of gratitude for what he'd received, but his demanding job as a director of Burmah-Castrol had prevented him. In his retirement years, the shop became an all-consuming interest.

Search as I will in the engagement diaries for those first years after his lung surgery, I can find no hint of recurring trouble. It was as if the cancer had never been. We celebrated our ruby wedding in July 1992; we spent holidays in Israel, Egypt and Portugal; we enjoyed our grandchild, Timothy, who had been born in June 1990. Frank, who had started using my diary for his engagements too, recorded his entries in a clear, confident hand. For the most part they concerned the shop; Mencap; meetings at the Castle School for the handicapped, of which he was a governor; discos for Nick; and, most Sundays, the car-boot sales to which he was addicted. When our second grandchild, Danielle, was born in March 1993, there was still no sign of anything wrong. The normally unexcitable Frank actually cheered when the news came that at last there was a girl in the family.

Only after June 1993 do I come across the first faint sign of trouble ahead: the word 'Physio' in the diary, suggesting that the pains in his back had started by then. On 13 September I read, 'Started steroid inhaler', and in January 1994 he records a session in a hydrotherapy pool. We were not unduly worried, especially as in that same month, a new lung specialist told Frank that he was likely soon to be off the danger list as far as cancer was concerned.

But when we joined some friends on a Caribbean cruise in February, Frank's breathlessness and lack of energy were cause for concern – he couldn't even manage a couple of circuits round the deck, and the least attempt at sightseeing left him shaking with exhaustion and looking for a taxi to take him back to the boat.

On the evening of 2 April, we went to a theatre in Bristol with our oldest son, Anthony, to see *Joseph and his Amazing Technicolour Dream Coat*. When Frank stood up at the end of the performance, he lost his balance and almost fell. After that, things deteriorated fairly rapidly. The dizziness became chronic in the weeks that followed – as did the backache, the breathlessness, an inability to concentrate, and pain in the prostate gland. He tried to ignore or laugh at the symptoms – though visits to osteopaths, chiropractors, acupuncturists and the like rapidly became a regular feature of his life. Then in July 1994, the situation changed irrevocably for the worse and I once again took up the writing of this diary.

Black Thursday. I have an ominous feeling that the entries that follow will be horribly significant, that is if I can bring myself to record them. I've had to force myself to start writing this morning, when the world has been turned upside down again and death is once more breathing down our necks. I have been pacing about the house like a caged animal, bursting into tears at frequent intervals. I'm getting morbid too: I've just picked up Frank's watch from the window-sill, and when I found it had stopped, the words of the corny old Grandfather Clock song – 'and it stopped short, never to go again, when the old man died' – kept playing themselves over and over in my head like a cracked record. Stupid and sentimental, but I can't help myself.

A week ago, we were still leading a more-or-less normal life. The symptoms had all been there, of course, but we had joked about them, putting them down to creeping senility. I'd even complained that he was stealing my thunder: after all, I'd always been the one with a long list of chronic ailments. Latterly, I'd begun to suspect him of hypochondria. Yes, I know it would have been completely out of character – he's never been one to fret about his health – but the Mencap shop has not been doing well recently, and he's not really had enough to occupy him. At all events, he didn't appear to be seriously incapacitated, and I felt able to return to India at the end of June, for several interviews with the Dalai Lama and various members of his family for the new book I was writing about them. Frank rang me once or twice in India to see how the interviews were coming along. He seemed cheerful and not particularly worried. But when he came to meet me at the airport on my return, he gave me the depressing news that the problem with his balance was getting worse.

Less than two weeks later, on the afternoon of 15 July, he had an appointment to see the lung specialist – mainly in order to get an all-clear for possible prostate surgery. (He was having trouble with his waterworks.) When Dr L (another doctor, different from Mr L) found a small growth on Frank's neck and suggested he went in to the clinic next day to have it removed, my first feeling was one of relief. Here perhaps was the source and explanation of all his troubles – if he had the lump removed, the symptoms would disappear with it. Frank saw the matter differently. For him, warning bells were clanging. 'You realise what this means, don't you?' he said quietly. 'The cancer may have returned.' Crazy though it may seem, the idea had simply not occurred to me! After all, had not Mr L assured him that the danger of cancer was receding?

The lump was bigger and went deeper than the surgeon had anticipated, and it took over an hour to remove under local anaesthetic. But when Frank came home later that Saturday, we were both optimistic that the immediate danger had been averted. That night he slept like a child.

The next night, however, was appalling. He was unable to pass water and had an intolerable pain in his bladder. At 3 a.m. he got up, put on a dressing-gown and paced round and round the garden. But there was no relief. He wondered aloud if he would ever learn to cope with such ghastly pain, and was very depressed. The following night he took a couple of pain-killers – so powerful that next morning he could hardly stand, his mouth was dry and he was very sick. The nights – and the sensible use of pain-killers – are going to be a problem.

I am determined to stay calm and supportive, as I know he would have been for me if our situations were reversed. We all have to die – I tell myself in a panicky way – death is an intrinsic part of life, programmed into it from the start.

'Men must endure their going hence, even as their coming hither. Ripeness is all,' and so on. All right, but taking the idea fully on board when I, like most other people, have usually preferred to run a mile from the thought of death, is quite another matter. There are no short-cuts, no magic wave of a wand to turn theory into acceptance. Though I know that self-pity is madness, I can feel it lurking in wait for me just around the corner. I'm desperately sad for Frank, but desperately sorry for me too. If the worst really does come to the worst, how shall I be able to face life without him? How will I manage to look after Nick? Frank's always been there for me; dependable in a crisis, commonsensical, caring. I need his unfailing support more than ever now when I'm knock-kneed with fright. Frank Longford has just rung and when I told him how I felt he reminded me that Dietrich Bonhoeffer in prison described himself as 'a contemptible, woebegone weakling'. That makes two of us then.

Later

Any small lingering hope was shattered when we saw Dr L. The look of grave sympathy on his face when we went into his office told us everything. 'Bad news, I'm afraid,' he said quietly, shuffling his papers. Frank reached for my hand; I squeezed his hard and took the deepest breath I could manage. The lump on his neck, went on Dr L, had proved malignant. The cancer had not, after all, gone away. It was still there in the lung and, even worse, had possibly spread to the brain and spine also. Our grip on each other's hands tightened to bone-cracking point as Frank nerved himself to ask the question that was tormenting both our minds – how much time did he have? Dr L could not be sure, of course, but thought six, maybe nine months. From the way he didn't quite look at us as he spoke the words, I knew we'd nothing to hope for.

I wonder how many times he's had to sit there handing out death sentences, watching people's lives shatter and explode in front of him. Does he ever get used to it? I suddenly thought back to that terrible day over thirty years ago, when a doctor had told me that our son, Paul, was profoundly mentally and physically abnormal, and had then walked off and left me to digest the information alone. Without a word of sympathy – or even a cup of tea.

Dr L was more considerate. Taking Frank off for the required blood tests and X-rays – it seemed to me that he was leading him away to the scaffold – he asked his secretary to get me some tea. By that time, he had already cut off all our escape routes. Nothing could be done, he had told us. Chemotherapy was largely a waste of time in the case of lung cancers and would involve a lot of extra angst for nothing. But, answering our next desperate question, he had assured us that the pain could be kept under control. I sipped the tea, thought of how everything had suddenly collapsed, and wondered how poor Frank was coping with his own fears and confusion.

What a strange irony that yesterday saw the launch of the first forty Hodder Christian Audiobooks, among them *Blessings*. I had done the audio-recording myself in May. Over the years, the book had struck a chord with people all over the world, some of whom claimed it had saved them from despair and suicide. There were many remarkable stories. When I came home last night, I looked up some of the many letters I'd received after its publication in 1979, and one of them leaped right off the page at me. 'Thank God for all the sadness out of which came comfort for so many,' someone had written. A week ago, I would have agreed, for the past was safely past. But now I felt a sudden chill. No, I wasn't prepared to thank God for the sadness; not now, not at this moment when it seemed all too likely that another tidal wave was poised to strike. The thought was unbearable and I wanted to scream out: 'No. Go away, leave me alone.'

Some people have imagined that I've become a kind of Superwoman; that in learning to live with having two mentally handicapped sons I must have emerged on to some sunlit plateau on which I am blessedly immune to further pain. 'How brave you are,' these unknown correspondents write. 'How I wish *I* could be like that', as if I had hit on some secret formula which is unavailable to anyone else, but which is mine for evermore. The image is so far from the truth that it makes me squirm. Coming to terms with reality is never easy; nothing in the world can ever make it so. We always have to do battle with our own detestation of change. I always was, am still and always will be a devout coward, collapsing in a heap at every fresh disaster, even minor ones; spending half my life worrying about things that may never happen. I confess that at times of acute depression, I have even been reduced to reading *Blessings* to see what it was I had once learned but seem to have forgotten. ('Wow,' I once found myself reacting. 'That's exactly it. Why didn't *I* think of that?!')

Today we appear to be back at the starting gate, waiting for the flag to fall. Back home – and how different everything now looks in the light of what we have just been told – Frank went to telephone Anthony, Mark, his older sister Kathleen, and Maureen, his twin. They were all as devastated as we were. We walked round the garden, doggedly admiring the glorious summer display and the shrubs that he has put in over the years, silently choking on the realisation that he will probably not be here to see them next time round. Later on – when my two friends, Anne and Sue, both phoned – I burst into tears. And this is only the first day!

Friday 29 July 1994

It's the commonest scenario in the world – every day millions die, and those who have loved them are left behind amid the wreckage of their lives. Why then do I feel this has never happened to anyone ever before, no one else has ever known this pain and terror? I should know better, considering the number of my Polish friends who suffered in Nazi or Soviet concentration camps and all the Tibetan friends who have gone through unspeakable horrors at the hands of the Chinese. And terrible things are happening every day in Rwanda, Bosnia, Peru, Iraq. Massacre, torture; hopeless and hungry people driven in terror from their homes, with nowhere else to go. And what about the poverty and deprivation here at home? And all the personal miseries by which people are so routinely crushed? I have never thought my own pain was unique or even special. I'm aware it's all a question of perspective. So why does now seem different? I'm fretting about one man dying from cancer, yet in the cruel, cold world out there millions would give their eye teeth for the chance of dying peacefully at home. Yes, but the difference is that the man dying of cancer is *my* man and the pain we're talking about is his pain and mine. We are all more vulnerable to the tragedies that actually invade our own lives.

I think of friends whose spouses have died of cancer – at the time, did I really appreciate how much pain they were going through? I try to remember how I responded. With suitable words of sympathy, I suppose: a card, flowers maybe, a lukewarm offer of help. Almost certainly not, I'm ashamed to say, the imaginative empathy which the situation called for. 'Those who are unhappy have no need for anything in this world but people capable of giving them their attention,' Simone Weil wrote somewhere.

But now it's my turn again. It is undeniably true that Time always heals in the end, but the time that comes in between the wound and its healing is just so bloody difficult to live through. I am in no mood for clichés. I am dissolving into nothingness, becoming anonymous, without identity. I pray for strength for us both, but find none. At this rate I'll be worse than useless to Frank, just when he needs me most. So far, it's *he* who is propping *me* up.

I know that every single human tragedy seems unique to the person going through it, but I must pull myself together, stop clinging to my own limited view of things. I try and concentrate on Erich Fromm's wise words, which I've so often quoted in talks and sermons:

> What we have gives us our identity, keeps us from drowning. It's only when circumstances unkindly let us down, when we are forced to watch our security dissolve, that we glimpse the truth that we have not really understood at all, that we've been trusting to the wrong things, pinning our happiness on what we have rather than on what we are. When the chips are down and we face the breakdown of what made life meaningful, we are plunged into the night.[5]

Into a night without stars.

Saturday 30 July 1994

The nights are worst for Frank – and therefore for me.

24

Yesterday, during the day, he felt better than he had for months and was amazingly cheerful. But when the painkiller effects wore off at about 3 a.m., his fears crowded in. 'I've such a long way to go with all this,' he gasped, and all I could do was put my arms round him and hold him tight, willing him to be consoled. Neither of us slept any more. He confessed to a feeling of panic that the cancer might have spread everywhere – to the spine, bowel and prostate, and possibly, most terrifying of all, to the brain. 'Any one of them would be terrible,' he sighed, 'but how am I going to bear all of them together?' I tried to comfort him, and it was then that I resolved to stop being so self-absorbed and concentrate on helping him hold his monstrous demons at bay.

Anthony came last night – terribly upset. He and Frank didn't always get on well together in the past, especially in the teenage years, but for many years now they've been very close, on the phone to each other most evenings. Anthony has come to depend a great deal on Frank's practical wisdom and common sense, and I have never seen him so distressed as now. After a bad night, which only Nick slept through, the three of us got up at 7 a.m. – the pain in Frank's back is slightly more bearable when he gets up and moves about. He and Anthony later took a load of books, clocks, bric-à-brac and oddments to the Mencap shop. We are already trying to unload some of our possessions.

Monday 1 August/Tuesday 2 August 1994

On Saturday we took a momentous decision: to look for a smaller house, with fewer stairs to climb and a less demanding garden. Luck in this instance was with us. We found one immediately, the first house we looked at; a fraction of the size of our present one, modern, compact, with only a small garden, exactly what we need. The negotiations will keep Frank busy and his mind occupied, and meanwhile I have to start on the task of throwing out much of the accumulated debris of over forty years. Thank goodness for the Mencap shop.

Yesterday I nearly came apart at the seams. Delayed action shock, I suppose. Post-traumatic stress disorder, or whatever they call it nowadays. (In 1958, a couple of weeks after we got the news about Paul's handicap, I woke up one morning to find myself totally unable to use my hands, to pick anything up, hold cutlery, etc. I can't remember how long it lasted, but I remember the sensation of utter bewilderment and helplessness.) This time round, I began having gasping, asthmatic, anxiety attacks. So much for the strength my *Blessings* admirers believe me to have – I am at present only able to grope for it blindly. I feel I'm back at square one again – but this time it's worse. (Does one always feel that? I suppose one invariably does.) In those terrible days when we discovered that two of our four sons were mentally handicapped, at least we had each other to turn to. Now one of us is going away. Oh hell, here come the tears. Self-pity's staging a comeback – in spades!

I consulted Lilian – one of the three GPs in our local group practice – about the panic attacks. She gave me some beta-blockers and came round after morning surgery to see Frank. Very sympathetic and reassuring, agreeing with Dr L that the pain could be kept under control. When she gave Frank some tablets with slow-release morphine we felt pleased. But when he took the first tablet, not only did it *not* relieve the pain but the back pains seemed worse than ever. In a panic later that evening, we rang Lilian at home. She said that unfortunately it was a question of trial and error; we'd get the dosage right in the end, but we'd have to be patient. Meanwhile, we could use our own aspirin-and-codeine tablets as a back-up. In spite of this, we had a disturbed night, with Frank in pain for much of it. It was dreadful – I couldn't even get him a drink because it has become so painful for him to pass water. Yet he will have to drink a lot of water to cope with the constipation which the tablets are already causing. What a vicious, vicious circle!

Maureen and Peter came over – his twin and his oldest friend. They were able to distract him more than I could and the house rang with laughter today. Maureen says we must try not to think about the future but concentrate on enjoying the time that remains. I'm well aware that she's trying to convince herself as much as us, but she's right, of course. Though we all know he can't enjoy anything much when he is in pain and his energy is seeping away, we have to try and keep him as cheerful as possible. Even if he only has a few months to live, that's still *months* – not just weeks or days. Be positive. (I have a disastrous tendency to think of a glass being half-empty, when the sensible course is to see it as still half-full. Isn't that the definition of a pessimist?)

I suddenly thought of that amazing TV interview Dennis Potter gave to Melvyn Bragg some months ago, when he was within weeks of dying. For years he had suffered from a painful and disabling psoriatic arthropathy, but the actual death sentence had been delivered for cancer of the pancreas, with secondaries already in the liver. Since the verdict, he had been working flat out to finish the play he was working on, pacing his room with pen at the ready, even though forced by pain to take frequent draughts from a hip-flask of liquid morphine. 'All I hope is that I'll have enough days left to finish it,' he told Bragg. Meanwhile – and this was what made the interview not just poignant but memorable – he was determined to live in the here-and-now. I scribbled a few notes as I listened, knowing before it began that this interview would be a priceless gem. (Almost twenty years earlier, I had myself gone to Potter's house in Ross-on-Wye to do a Radio 4 interview with him and it proved so spellbinding that the *Listener* printed it almost verbatim.) 'Yesterday is in us,' he now said, 'but it's not here in front of us, and tomorrow is unpredictable. The only thing we have for sure is now. I celebrate now.' (He had spoken to me along these lines too, adding that the ability to live in the present implied 'an immense trust in the order of things'.) There followed one of the loveliest, gentlest paeans of praise for the Now that I have ever heard. 'Below my window there's a plum-tree, with the whitest, frothiest, blossomiest blossom that there ever could be.' Potter was overcome with delight at the contemplation of this image, though his face was drawn and he was forced to take yet another swig from the flask of morphine. 'The now-ness of everything is absolutely wondrous,' he said. 'When you see the present tense, boy, do you see it! And you celebrate.'

Within a few weeks of uttering that final testament, this master word-spinner was dead. But he had finished his play – and hadn't he told us that once he'd finished it he'd be ready to go? What a man! And – despite the abuse hurled at him by some of our moralists – what a powerful force for good! Dennis Potter thought deeply about good and evil and about the nature of ultimate reality and, though his plays were unpalatable to many (often including myself), his insights were as profound as they were troubling and he never trivialised life. I can't honestly remember now whether it was in the interview with me (I think it was) or in the later Lent talk Gerry Priestland asked him to do for Radio 4 that he used this memorable passage which is in my private anthology of favourite pieces:

The world is being made right in front of us and we stand

always at the cutting edge of this creation and in living out our lives give back piece by piece what has been given to us, to use and work with and wrestle with. We shape our own lives and find our own humanity in the long passage from premonitions of innocence through the darkness of moral distress, carelessness and apparent absurdity into the light that we know is there, if we have the patience and the courage to be still, to concentrate and to be alert.

Yet this man stands accused of blasphemy! I owe a great debt of gratitude to Dennis Potter – to me he was a great teacher, a free spirit who was faithful to his vocation. 'What I do is me; for that I came,' as the poet said.

Nor must I forget Ken Thomas, a local Berkshire hero who, from the moment he learned that he had terminal cancer – it too was in the liver – spent his last remaining months careering round the county to raise funds for the new CT scanner at the Royal Berks Hospital – the one, in fact, that Frank has just been through. Frank and I were deeply impressed by what we saw of Ken and his wife, Polly; and Richard Ingrams got the editor of the *Sunday Telegraph* colour supplement to commission me to write an article about them. Two inspiring people.

Why can't I be like them instead of just admiring them? What is it with me?

I think back to one of my recent visits to Dharamsala in India, when my friend Brigid Marlin and I were discussing the subject of free will with two young doctors from California. I can hear myself quoting from Viktor Frankl's wonderful book, *Man's Search for Meaning*, which Brigid and I both loved: 'The last and greatest of the human freedoms – the ability to choose one's attitude.' That is what Dr Frankl discovered amid the horror of the Nazi concentration camps

– the one area of freedom which no power on earth can ever take from us:

> We who lived in concentration camps can remember the men who walked through huts comforting others, giving away their last piece of bread. They may have been few in number, but they offer sufficient proof that everything can be taken from a man but one thing: the last of the human freedoms – to choose one's attitude in any given set of circumstances, to choose one's own way ... He may retain his human dignity even in a concentration camp. Dostoievsky said once, 'There is only one thing I dread: not to be worthy of my sufferings.' These words frequently came to my mind after I became acquainted with those martyrs whose behaviour in camp, whose suffering and death, bore witness to the fact that the last inner freedom cannot be lost. It can be said that they were worthy of their sufferings; the way they bore their suffering was a genuine inner achievement. It is this spiritual freedom – which cannot be taken away – that makes life meaningful and purposeful.[6]

I am utterly convinced that we must learn to live with those tragedies in our lives which are unavoidable (the avoidable ones, of course, are a different matter). What ultimately matters is not what life so wantonly throws at us, but what we make of it – whether we continue to act like loving human beings within our changed circumstances, learning from them, growing with them, turning them resolutely towards good. I believe that there is no evil from which good cannot be brought.

Nevertheless, when one is hurting, even the most deeply held beliefs can seem to count for nothing. Mired in pain, we shun every approach of wisdom. It is easier – when the pain is new and raw – to be a rebel, to scream inwardly, to rage against the unfairness of it all. I'm screaming inside now. It is intolerable to think that Frank's life is going to be snuffed out, while the world goes on as before, as if nothing had changed. At supper, Peter talked about their plans for next year, and it was like a knife going through my heart. (Clichés again!)

Thursday 4 August 1994

I let off steam writing this journal – and console myself reading books, whenever I find the time. (Actually, I don't find much.) Last night in bed I dipped into Sogyal Rinpoche's *Tibetan Book of Living and Dying*. All the great religious traditions have their own special light to shed on the basic truths about life. In the Eastern tradition – whether in India, Tibet, China, Japan, Burma, Thailand or Sri Lanka – there is less running away from reality than in our own, more stress on finding and developing the real self, more acceptance of pain, disappointment, failure and death as part of the very fabric of existence. In recent years, much wisdom on the subject of death has been offered to the West by exiled Tibetan sages, who insist on reminding us of the impermanence of all things material. Sogyal Rinpoche writes:

> I ask myself often 'Why is it that everything changes?' And only one answer comes back to me: That is how life is. Nothing, nothing at all, has any lasting character . . . One of the chief reasons we have so much anguish and difficulty facing death is that we ignore the truth of impermanence. We so desperately want everything to continue as it is that we have to believe that things will

always stay the same. But this is only make-believe . . . it has little or nothing to do with reality. This make-believe, with its misinformation, ideas and assumptions, is the rickety foundation on which we construct our lives. No matter how the truth keeps interrupting, we prefer to go on trying, with hopeless bravado, to keep up our pretence.

In our minds changes always equal loss and suffering. And if they come, we try to anaesthetize ourselves as far as possible. We assume, stubbornly, and unquestioningly, that permanence provides security and impermanence does not. But, in fact, impermanence is like some of the people we meet in life – difficult and disturbing at first, but on deeper acquaintance far friendlier and less unnerving than we could have imagined.

Life may be full of pain, suffering and difficulty, but all of these are opportunities handed to us to help us move toward an emotional acceptance of death. It is only when we believe things to be permanent that we shut off the possibility of learning from change.

If we shut off this possibility, we become closed, and we become grasping. Grasping is the source of all our problems. Since impermanence to us spells anguish, we grasp on to things desperately, even though all things change. We are terrified of letting go, terrified, in fact, of living at all, since learning to live is learning to let go. And this is the tragedy and the irony of our struggle to hold on: not only is it impossible, but it brings us the very pain we are seeking to avoid.[7]

Wonderful stuff, but change is nevertheless hell to contend with and absorb. It is now next morning and we have been thrown back into the melting-pot, not knowing any longer how things stand. We have just returned from the hospital where we were stunned to learn that the latest X-rays show no sign of cancer anywhere. There must be some somewhere – the biopsy proved that – but it now seems unlikely that Frank is riddled with it. It's all very perplexing. They have been praying for Frank at our church for the last several weeks. Do I now have to tell them to stop, that it was a false alarm? Do we start hoping again? If so, what do we hope for? Actually, Dr L put things firmly in perspective when I asked him what this new information meant for us. 'It may mean that he has a year to live, rather than months,' he said. So nothing's changed very much.

Madeleine, the Macmillan nurse, made her first visit this afternoon and reinforced that view: 'Secondaries are second-aries,' she said firmly, 'and they are incurable.' But, like the others, she insisted that Frank mustn't worry too much about the pain; it would not be allowed to get out of hand, she said reassuringly. Meanwhile it was important for us to enjoy the time that was left to us. We were entering a period of 'quality time', she said, and must make the most of it. Despite the depressing circumstances in which we were making her acquaintance, we took to Madeleine instantly and were relieved to feel that we were in capable hands.

Tuesday 9 August 1994

It's like being on the big dipper. Good things and bad swoop down with stupefying speed. Frank is now in hospital. He continued to have a lot of pain at night and was finding it agonising to pass water. Neither of us was getting any sleep. Last Friday he went to see a urologist in Oxford (we're almost losing track of the numerous and varied specialists he has consulted) who promised to get him into hospital as soon as possible. Three ghastly nights later, we were becoming desperate. Yesterday morning, after a particularly pain-racked one, Tracey Maleham drove Frank to the Royal Berks Hospital in Reading for a brain scan. While he was away, I rang the urologist, begging him to hurry things up. As a result, within a couple of hours of Frank's return his old youth club friend, Gerard Gibbons (now a near neighbour in Newbury), had come to take him to the Acland Hospital in Oxford. (I was supposed to be having a cataract operation myself next week, but have rung the hospital to ask them to put it on hold. Ironically, it was Frank who, last April, after we discovered that I had cataracts on both eyes, had urged me to have the operation. I had wanted to put it off until after I had finished my current book on Tibet. But he had insisted. 'No,' he said, 'you must have it done sooner rather than later. I want to be around to look after you.' I had burst into tears at this, having no idea till then that he suspected his days were numbered. It was the first time he had hinted at it.)

Last evening a young couple came, unexpectedly, to view our house, which was about to be put on the market but had not yet been publicly advertised. News travels fast. The timing could not have been worse. Frank was in hospital, everywhere was in a mess, the loo in one of the bathrooms had sprung a leak and I was waiting for the plumber to come and fix it. In fact, when I saw their car arrive, I thought they *were* the plumber, which was why I rushed outside to greet them with such enthusiasm. Still, they had come a long way and were so eager to look round that I relented. Thank God I did. They fell in love with the house instantly, mess or no mess, and, despite the flooded bathroom, rushed straight down to the estate agents to say they wanted to buy it. Amid all the ghastliness, the house buying-and-selling is proving to be a piece of cake. At least something is going well for us.

Last night too, Frank was told by the urologist that the

brain scan was negative. No cancer of the brain, then. Eureka! And today he came successfully through the prostatectomy. Can things be looking up?

The *Tibetan Book of Living and Dying* imposes its own calm perspective. Sogyal writes of a woman who came to see his teacher one day. 'My doctor has given me only a few months to live. Can you help me? I'm dying.' To her surprise the teacher began to chuckle. Then he said quietly, 'We are all dying. It's only a matter of time. Some of us just die sooner than others.'

Wednesday 10 August 1994

My friend Anne and her husband Mike drove me to Oxford to see Frank – I am forbidden to drive because of my wretched eyesight – and we found him looking quite perky after the op. Later in the day, however, the catheter began to cause him excruciating pain. When I rang in the early evening, he was in such agony that he couldn't even speak, could only gasp out how atrocious the pain was. It was very upsetting, but some hours later, just as I had decided that I really would have to turn in and get some sleep if he didn't ring soon, he rang to say that the catheter had been removed and he was feeling a lot better.

Trevor Dorey, the Anglican curate in the village and a close friend, called round and I showed him a passage I'd rediscovered in my Carlo Carretto anthology. I'd completely forgotten its existence and had just come upon it by accident. Carretto says:

> The point is to learn how to suffer with love. So many people suffer with hatred in their hearts . . . But he who suffers with love has the power to save the world . . . The

Christian does not reason like the Marxist, that one day there will be no more diseases, no more earthquakes, no more pain. He knows that there will always be a pit for people to fall into. We have to fill in as many pits as possible, yet never forget that there will always be a pit especially for me, and in it I must come to understand the mystery of the Cross, which will lead me to resurrection . . .[8]

Wednesday 31 August 1994

We haven't moved very far in the last two weeks, except that Enid and David (two of my childhood friends from St Helens), very concerned about what is happening and casting round for ways in which to help Frank, have put him in touch with their son-in-law, Raoul Coombes, who is Professor of Oncology at Charing Cross Hospital. We have an appointment to see Raoul – positively our last hope – on Friday. We are no nearer finding the cause of Frank's lack of balance or breathlessness or exhaustion, and he's not at all sure the prostatectomy has actually worked – the waterworks problem is as bad as ever.

There was an article in yesterday's *Times* by a woman whose mother had died a very distressing death from cancer. I began to read, then lost my nerve, couldn't go on reading, threw the paper down, walked away from it. Yet I knew damned well the article was still there and the awareness of it haunted me all day; it tormented me and drew me, like a magnet with iron filings. (I used to be just as much of a coward over articles about the nuclear bomb!) I was forced to realise that however much I may want to make my 'Yes' of acceptance, I am very far from that point. 'Yes', as long as I am allowed to write the script myself. Otherwise, a loud – and terrified – 'No!'

Tuesday 6 September 1994

Roy Castle died a few days ago after a long fight against lung cancer. Afterwards Fiona, his wife, said there should be no sadness for his death, only joy. If only I had so much faith and courage. Some people make one feel ashamed.

Raoul has admitted Frank into the Charing Cross Hospital for tests, scans, etc. My school-friend, Margaret, has come to stay, so that I don't have to be on my own.

Margaret, Nick and I went to see the film of *Shadowlands* tonight at the Corn Exchange, and I found it unbearably poignant. (I can't imagine what poor Nick made of it, but I think he enjoyed having an evening out.) It brought home the astonishing gulf between the C. S. Lewis who had written *The Problem of Pain* – the rather complacent academic, sure of his faith, with an answer for every 'problem' – and the humbler, vulnerable Lewis of *A Grief Observed*, torn asunder by grief for his dead wife, aware now that there are no answers, only a deep abiding mystery. When I read both books twenty years or so ago, I honestly don't think I noticed much difference. I shall reread them tonight, if I can find them on the bookshelves.

Thursday 8 September 1994

Brought Frank out of Charing Cross by taxi. The only cancer to be found was in a gland near the lump which Dr L had removed in July. It was small and thankfully dormant. Raoul said they wouldn't do anything about it now, but would scan the gland at regular intervals. If it should become active, radiation therapy might be required. It sounded a relatively upbeat diagnosis.

But after Frank came home, it was downhill all the way.

His balance went haywire; he had caught some sort of bug in the hospital ward and had frightful diarrhoea; his waterworks seized up again; and he was in a lot of pain. I called the GP, who diagnosed an infection and prescribed a course of antibiotics. Frank meanwhile went off to have a bath.

Suddenly I heard a yell. I rushed upstairs to find him shouting for help. Though he had managed to get into the bath, he was quite incapable of getting out of it. But I couldn't help him. Struggle as I would, I could not shift him an inch. Margaret had run upstairs after me, and I called her in. Between us, we heaved him out of the bath, wrapped him in a couple of towels and, putting one of his arms around each of us, pushed and pulled him back into bed. I don't know which of the three of us was most exhausted.

Poor Nick had come upstairs to see what the trouble was and he had grown increasingly agitated. He kept saying, 'What's happening to Dad? Tell me', while tears rolled down his cheeks. Margaret and I hugged him tight and told him as best we could, but it was difficult to find the right words, and I'm not sure how successful we were. Poor Nick. He knows something is badly wrong with his Dad, but he doesn't as yet understand what it all means. I'm sure he finds it very distressing.

Friday 16 September 1994

Went to see Lilian at the surgery. I went in first. When Frank joined me, she looked at us both for a long time in silence, then said, '*Your* strength is in each other.'

Monday 19 September 1994

Once again by taxi to Charing Cross, this time for a broncho-scopy. The bronchoscopy – involving tubes down the throat – was a nightmare experience, and Frank said afterwards that if he'd known how awful it would be he'd have refused point-blank to have it. We're getting sick to death of hos-pitals, yet there's no escaping them. We have to go back again to Charing Cross on Wednesday for the results of the bronchoscopy and for some kind of tests on the nerve-ends of his fingers and toes.

Wednesday 21 September 1994

Tests on the fingers and toes this morning at Charing Cross. We had thought they would be fairly routine and were not unduly worried. But we could tell immediately from the neurologist's reaction that we were not going to like the results. Before we left for home, a Dr Lim (we hadn't seen him before) told us that the bronchoscopy had revealed the airways to be narrowed and inflamed though not completely blocked. He didn't pull any punches. The lung cancer had spread into the system, he said, and nothing could halt its advance. Chemotherapy would be a waste of time. In the short term, however, steroids should help to improve the quality of Frank's life. Less palatable was the news that from now on he must walk with a stick.

Raoul joined us and confirmed that they had run out of options. We reminded him about this morning's nerve-ending tests, and he rang for the results. His face was grave as he put the phone down and turned to look at us. Our hearts sank and once again we reached for each other's hands. The loss of balance, the tingling in the legs, the breathlessness – Raoul told us – are all now confirmed beyond doubt as cancer-related.

It's the worst news so far. But shocks are part of our lives now and we were able to be reasonably sanguine about this latest one. I looked back in these pages and found again that quotation from *Good Friday People*. It's so very relevant now to read: 'We, without a future . . . knowing that nothing is safe . . .'

Friday 23 September 1994

Madeleine, our Macmillan nurse, came in today. We didn't ask her to give us any hope, because we know there isn't any. She warned us of some of the possible side-effects of taking steroids – fluid retention, papery skin, putting on weight and so on. She says Frank won't notice any difference for about ten days, but after that he should begin to feel – and look – markedly better. That is something to look forward to, as at present he has no energy at all and the very least movement exhausts him. Madeleine suggests that he should use two sticks rather than just one, and warns that before long it'll be a question of a zimmer frame. Gloomy prospect. 'Don't try to fight this by yourself,' she says, 'leave it to the Holy Spirit.'

I went upstairs to the bathroom, locked the door and cried my heart out. I understand why some people want to shriek, 'Why me?', but I won't, won't, won't go down that path. After all, why *not* me? The world grows through the process of change and decay, and everything and everyone within it is subject to the same physical laws. But I cling to my belief that the facts are ultimately friendly: there is no evil in the world which cannot be touched by grace. 'It seems to me,' says Siddhartha, in Hermann Hesse's remarkable

novel of that name, 'that everything that exists is good –
death as well as life, sin as well as holiness, folly as well as
wisdom. Everything is necessary, everything needs only my
agreement, my assent, my loving understanding; then all
is well with me and nothing can harm me.'[9]

So not, quite definitely *not*, why me? More realistically,
'So, if that's the way it is, how am I going to live with it, for
live with it I must?' We all take our chances, and each of us
must one day confront our own mortality. Right, I tell myself
firmly. Dry your eyes, blow your nose, go downstairs – and
face the situation exactly as it is. Neither minimise nor
exaggerate. Accept that at present and for the foreseeable
future, things are not going your way. Don't fight it. Just *be*!
I recall a consoling image in one of Chögyam Trunggpa's
books, about compassion being like a moon shining in the
sky while its image is reflected in a hundred bowls of water.

> The moon does not demand, 'If you open to me, I will do
> you a favour and shine on you.' The moon just shines
> . . .There is no audience involved, no 'me' and 'them'. It is
> a matter of an open gift, complete generosity without the
> relative notions of giving and receiving. That is the basic
> openness of compassion: opening without demand.
> Simply be what you are, be the master of the situation. If
> you will just 'be', then life flows around and through you.[10]

Nick arrived home today from an adventure holiday in
Wales organised by his day centre. We miss him dreadfully
when he goes away, and were rather apprehensive about
the 'adventure' aspect of the holiday. Nick is neither athletic
nor adventurous, and on the whole he's not keen on exerting
himself. We need not have worried, however, because he
was glowing with excitement when he came back. He was
bursting to tell us all about it: he had been canoeing and

sailing (fell in and got soaked three times, he said proudly); had done pony-trekking, archery, abseiling and – obviously the highlight of the entire trip – had been to the pub every evening for a G and T! (So that's where all his money went!) He'd loved every minute of it and wanted to know when he could go again.

He eyed Frank apprehensively though, wanting him to be back to normal; his eyes followed him every time he went out of the room. Nick simply hates it when things are not as they should be; he's a stickler for routine and for everything being in its proper place. A born conservative. Incredible to think that up to a few short months ago, Frank and I were dancing (like a couple of demented hippos) with Nick every evening at bedtime – night after night, month after month, year after year, on our own or with friends – two records: the first always the latest chart-topper; the second one always Shakin' Stevens' 'Lipstick, Powder and Paint'. We seemed to have been doing it since time began, and could not imagine an evening that was disco-less at its end. Nor could Nick. It was a terrible blow for him when his Dad suddenly became too tired to take part in this nightly ritual. He simply couldn't understand it.

Wednesday 5 October 1994

Poor old Nick caught an ear infection as a result of all those drenchings in mid-Wales, and by Monday he was completely deaf. He was put on antibiotics, but naturally enough was very unhappy. He never has much hearing – none at all in the right ear – and to lose what little he has is sheer misery for him. Fortunately, the inflammation had subsided by Saturday and I was able to start putting drops in his ear. On Monday, he had it syringed and his hearing mercifully returned. (A look of ecstasy comes over his face at that moment. He thanks the doctor enthusiastically and nearly pumps his hand off. Colin West always says he's never known such a grateful patient.)

One of the staff from Nick's day centre rang to say they were going to start talking to him about moving to the new house, and asked if they should broach the subject of Frank's illness at the same time. It seems quite a good idea, though it's not easy to get Nick to engage in discussion on any topic but television. He's lazy when it comes to words. If you ask him a question, you can see him hoping that if he keeps quite still it will go away and stop bothering him.

Frank's former boss, Peter Maynard, has been over from Ecuador, where he and his wife, Maruja, now live. He rang last Sunday from London to say, 'Sorry to miss you, see you next year', but when he discovered how things stood with Frank he came down on an early train next morning. Down on one train, and back on the next one. We were very touched. A couple of days later, we got a letter from him. We both seemed, he wrote, 'to be living in the grace of God'. It was some consolation for the vacuum I feel inside, the sense of God's absence. Perhaps we are not the best judges of our own spiritual state.

After two weeks, the steroids seem to have had little effect, except that Frank is fractionally less breathless. Everything else is still tormenting him: the lack of balance, loss of energy, the backache, the prostate trouble – what a catalogue of woes! 'I hate idling around while you're rushed off your feet,' he says feelingly. No one could ever have called Frank an idler. He was always busy, always had his long checklist of jobs to be done – whether it was the garden, the car, the garage, defrosting the freezer, changing plugs and washers, mending the boiler or, on at least two occasions in the past, putting in an entire central-heating system. He was not in any way a craftsman, but as a do-it-yourselfer he had no equal. Clearly he loathes his present enforced inactivity, but he is astonishingly uncomplaining. When I told him yesterday how much I admired this new-found patience, he said, 'Well, I can only manage to stay that way because of you.' Another weepy moment.

The key to learning to live in the present moment is letting go of the past, but where do we find the courage to let go? We seem manically determined to hang on to what is transient, passing, changing, rather than see what is eternal in ourselves and in our world. (Wasn't it Plato who said we should turn away with our whole souls from the things which pass?) The true essence of Frank, the divine spark – the 'Buddha nature' – within him, the love that binds us together, those are imperishable. But as for our material selves, our circumstances and our surroundings, the only certainty is change: nothing stays as it is. Life's fleeting phenomena will not stay for us; we must learn to wave them goodbye.

Thursday 20 October 1994

Frank waved goodbye to an important part of his life tonight, when he handed over all the Mencap shop papers to Pat Slater, chairman of Newbury Mencap. Pat came to the house with Edna Wall who is taking over the accounts. It was an emotional occasion, perhaps the first of many goodbyes. I know Frank felt it keenly, and the other two, who had worked with him for some years, went away not trusting themselves to speak.

Wednesday 26 October 1994

Frank has gone to Charing Cross, for a bone scan at 10 a.m. He can scarcely stand unaided now and really can't be left alone for a moment. Raoul, when we saw him on Monday, was obviously shocked by the rapid deterioration in his condition. He wondered if perhaps they had been looking in the wrong direction, particularly as the CT scan last week showed that the originally identified cancer cell was still dormant. But *something* clearly is far from dormant. As the neuropathy – the nerve paralysis that is slowly creeping up his body – is known to be cancer-related, perhaps there's an undiscovered cancer somewhere else which is galloping. Hence the bone scan, the only area so far unscanned. The neurologist is being called in, and once again it means an overnight stay in hospital.

It does seem crazy at a time like this, but we are in the throes of house removal. Actually, it has been the best possible thing for both of us, as it takes our minds off more unpleasant realities. Even though he is incapable of any actual physical work, Frank has been able to sit and make telephone calls, arrange for different jobs to be done, pay bills, order supplies and so on. The new house is now ours and we have workmen in all the time. Despite the ban on my driving, I keep taking car-loads of stuff up there and am gradually filling cupboards and shelves. The old house begins to look desolate, unloved, abandoned. But I have never been sentimental about houses, and I'll be glad to go.

Thursday 17 November 1994

Almost a month has passed since I last wrote in this journal. I have been so busy there has simply been no time. We have now moved house, and, thank God, it is much much better – for us all and especially for Frank. The other place had become impossible. Here, in a smaller, compact, less rambling and more efficiently heated house, he can move around at least a little. The distances from A to B are not so large. As for Nick, he is thrilled with the move, and when I took him up that first day to show him his new bed-sitting-room, fitted out with cupboards, and with his own television, video and music centre, he was over the moon. 'I jus' doan believe it,' he said excitedly over and over again when the mini-bus brought him back from the day centre, 'It's marbellous.' So 'marbellous', in fact, that we scarcely see him now except when he deigns to come downstairs and join us for meals. Frank is rather sad about this, as in the other house he was always with us. But I think it is good that Nick is discovering a new sense of independence and is happy with it.

Frank's condition, alas, continues to get worse. It's not the cancer that's killing him, it seems, but the neuropathy. He can no longer walk; except painfully, a very little, with two sticks. If we go out (which we do only rarely), we have to put a wheelchair in the car – and it's surprisingly heavy to lift in and out. He can do nothing now but sit and make phone calls and write a few letters in handwriting which has become alarmingly shaky and illegible. Everything – particularly getting out of his chair to make his slow and painful way to the loo – exhausts him.

A few weeks ago I recorded that he was to have a bone scan. It was negative like all the others. But Raoul had simultaneously ordered a lumbar puncture, and this revealed – at long last – an active cancer in the spinal fluid. Frank rang me from the hospital, actually quite relieved that something positive had at last come to light. Raoul, he said, was cautiously optimistic. Now that he knew what he was dealing with, a course of six lumbar punctures plus six injections of chemotherapy might possibly see off the cancer cells and restore Frank to normal living. With this hope – and it really did seem a genuine one – we postponed having a stair-lift put in. Suddenly there was the possibility that he might walk again.

Once a week since then Frank has gone off to Hammersmith for his chemotherapy. Today is the fourth time and so far there's no obvious improvement. The neuropathy continues its unstoppable progress upwards, the tingling having now reached above the waist. Last night I could see he had lost hope. I don't know how to comfort him. How do you calm another's anguish and terror? How do you help, except by letting them know that you love them, and that you are in this together as far as is humanly possible?

Thursday 24 November 1994

Frank has been back in Charing Cross all this past week. The chemotherapy, clearly not working, has been discontinued. Yesterday he was taken to Chertsey to have an all-over, top-to-toe scan which took two and a half hours. He has just rung me to say that the scan has revealed two cancerous nodules in the spinal column. So now there is talk of radiotherapy.

Sunday 4 December 1994

Raoul lost no time. Radiotherapy treatment began on Friday, and this week Frank is to go every day to Charing Cross. Since the first session the pain has actually been worse and his exhaustion total. (How total is total?) But to some extent, given the stress of the long double journey, that was to be expected. But he is very patient and uncomplaining.

We've suddenly wakened up to the fact that there'll be no one to look after me after the cataract operation, postponed from August and now scheduled for next Friday. Apparently I will not be able to cope without help, as I shan't be allowed to bend down or lift anything. So, as he can't help me himself, Frank has telephoned an organisation called Oxford Aunts and arranged for one of the Aunts to come and live in for a week.

Meanwhile we have re-ordered the stair-lift. (We're getting a reconditioned, half-price one). Getting up and down the stairs has become almost impossible for him. In the other house, of course, he would long since have had to admit defeat.

Tuesday 13 December 1994

Our son Mark's birthday. I don't suppose it'll be a very happy one for him.

I had my cataract op. a few days ago and still can't see very well. In fact, I'm almost as blind as the proverbial bat, but I must peer at the paper and try and keep this journal going. When I came out of the Hampshire Clinic, Sue came round to cook the meal and she and Desmond shared it with us and stayed to wash up. (We have such wonderful friends. Sue always reminds me of Kanga, the character in *Winnie-the-Pooh* who 'knows a good thing to do and does it'. Unassuming, practical kindness at all times.) Next morning, Kit Gunn arrived, the Oxford Aunt who is to look after the three of us for a week. She seems very pleasant and efficient, so I shall sit back gratefully and let her take over.

This morning, Frank went off for his seventh radiotherapy session. He came back as usual just before one o'clock and sat down at the kitchen table. I asked him how things had gone, and he opened his mouth to say 'OK' or something of the sort. Instead he put his head in his hands and wept. (Kit tactfully withdrew.) 'It's no good,' he said blankly, as he tried to pull himself together. It was heartbreaking. In the almost fifty years I have known him, it's the first time I've ever seen him weep. He was always the strong unflappable one; he had to be, given my frequent massive collapses of self-confidence. But now he was the one who was lost. I held him tight and cried too. Francis Thompson's lines flashed into my mind,

> But (when so sad thou canst not sadder)
> Cry; – and upon thy so sore loss,
> Shall shine the traffic of Jacob's ladder,
> Pitched betwixt Heaven and Charing Cross.[11]

At Charing Cross this morning they had told him that the radiotherapy obviously wasn't working, and they had nothing more to offer. I don't know whether it was this sudden removal of hope, or the fact that he had to come home and break the news to me, that had caused him to break down. Whatever the cause, it was a deeply painful moment. 'So sad thou canst not sadder.'

I slipped out of the room to ring our friends, Mike and Anne, and asked them to come over this afternoon. I think Mike's reassuring presence will be good for Frank. They came straight over, by which time Frank had recovered some of his aplomb. He gave Anne a silver fountain-pen which someone had given him long ago. Knowing what I'd just told her, she burst into tears and put her arms round him. I don't think he really understood why she was crying.

Well, it's reappraisal time again. We came to terms with the original state of affairs when it hit us some months ago, and now we must do so again. Why isn't it possible to do so once and for all when trouble first strikes? Why do we always have to keep picking ourselves up and starting again from the beginning? I suppose it is because hope will insist on springing eternal and then we drop our guard. Once again we had been clutching at straws – we'd sent out a couple of hundred Christmas letters to friends – (well, two hundred copies of one letter), saying how hopeful we were about the radiotherapy. (Actually, in drafting the letter, I had typed that we had 'great hopes' of it, but Frank had made me change that to 'some small hope'.) But that was then, and this is now. The markers are being called in.

Wednesday 14 December 1994

Last night when he got into bed (an obstacle-course hurdle which is unbelievably difficult for him) Frank said, 'I think that a fortnight from now I'll be bedridden.' He was quite matter-of-fact about it; there was no self-pity in the statement. But there it was. We slept fitfully. This morning he was resolutely cheerful, but he composed a note for me to fax through to Raoul, suggesting that if Raoul wanted to see him again it ought to be sooner rather than later, as later might well be too late. He won't be able to undertake the journey to Hammersmith for much longer. He ended the note, 'It looks as though we have lost the battle, Raoul, but I'm grateful to you for trying so hard to win it.' He then set about writing his personal Christmas cards, something he'd never in his life done willingly.

It does feel awfully like coming up to the last days. When he struggled up to bed for a rest he said, 'I can't go on doing this much longer.' He is scared I won't be able to continue looking after him at home and he hates the thought of dying in hospital. But I have told him that I am determined to keep him here and look after him. I expect Madeleine and Jenny, the district nurse, will help me through.

Christmas cards and letters are coming in thick and fast. I thought I'd find them distressing, but they are in fact very comforting, full of affection and encouragement. One friend quoted Scott Fitzgerald: 'Often we write to certain people that we "think of you all the time". We lie, of course, but not entirely. For they are always with us, a few of them, so deep in us that they are part of us. Sometimes they are indeed the marrow of our bones, so if they die they live on in us.' All of the cards implore us not to lose hope. Prayers are promised from all quarters: people have contacted the Tyburn nuns, the Carmelites, the Ursulines and the Franciscan Missionaries to pray for us. All our friends hope that the Christmas blessings for 1994 will 'exceed our expectations'. Some wish they were nearer to help or to visit in person. Some have their own tale of woe: one friend sends the horrifying news that his daughter (to whom I taught French and Latin in the first form many years ago in Bowdon) now has cancer and is undergoing chemotherapy.

Malcolm Brenton (whose wife was my friend, Sue Turner, formerly head of children's programmes at Thames TV, who died of cancer last year) had been none too keen on the allusions to prayer in the letter we had sent out, but hoped they meant we were doing some positive thinking. (They did, Malcolm, they did.) Malcolm and Sue were atheists, with their own special wisdom. 'Spend your time saying thankyou and sorry,' he wrote now. 'It helps if you start with only a few regrets – but continue to work on those so that there are none. We once went to a very peculiar wedding where guests were asked to give "spiritual" presents. I wrote them a poem, which Sue performed:

> If it was your fault – I forgive you
> Life is too short
> for debating whose fault it was.
> Saying thankyou is so much easier.

His words struck a chord – Frank and I *had* already talked over the past, forgiven each other for past hurts and failures and said thankyou for the many good things.

His letter, says Malcolm, is what Sue would have wanted to send, 'plain, commonsensical heathen support and comfort'. I couldn't help but think what a burden of mis-understanding is carried by weasel words like 'heathen' and 'atheist' – and, for that matter, 'God'. A 'heathen' finds the divine at work in nature, an 'a-theist' rejects the theistic definition of ultimate reality. I cannot fault either of them. I often think we Judaeo-Christians have caused havoc with our concept of an almighty, judgmental, legalistic and often vengeful God, made in our own image and likeness rather than the other way round. To me God is a mystery hidden in a great 'cloud of unknowing', and as the poet, R. S. Thomas, put it,

> God . . . that great absence
> In our lives, the empty silence
> Within, the place where we go
> Seeking, not in hope to
> Arrive or find.[12]

But if I were to attempt a more positive definition, I would say that God is the presence and possibility of unselfish love in our lives and in our flawed world; the indescribable, inexpressible ultimate reality, which permeates all that exists, which is within and all about us. Does it really matter whether we refer to the ground of our being as God, as

Brahma, as the Tao (the way), as Sunyata (emptiness) or as Al Haqq (the reality)? We ought not to forget that awareness of God (as distinct from gods) was born in India in the middle of the sixth century BC – before the Old Testament prophets and Patriarchs – and that the *Upanishads* (Breath of the Eternal) were the first sacred writings the world had ever seen.

My imagination is profoundly stirred by some of the definitions of God found in the older, Eastern sacred texts; this, from the *Upanishads*, for example:

> Thou art imperishable.
> Thou art the changeless Reality.
> Thou art the source of life.

And:

> Thou alone art – thou the Light
> Imperishable, adorable:
> Great Glory is thy name.
> No one equal to thee.[13]

Krishna in the *Bhagavad Gita* says, no less emphatically:

> I am the reality that abides
> in the soul of all creatures,
> And of all creatures I am
> the beginning, middle and end.[14]

'Hidden deep but ever present', we find in the *Tao Te Ching*:

> Something mysteriously formed,
> Born before heaven and earth.
> In the silence and the void,

Standing alone and unchanging,
Ever present and in motion.
Perhaps it is the mother of ten thousand things.
I do not know its name.
Call it Tao.
For lack of a better word, I call it great.[15]

And what of the Sikh morning prayer which begins with
the words:

There is one God,
Eternal Truth is His Name;
Maker of all things,
Fearing nothing and at enmity with nothing,
Timeless is His Image;
Not begotten, being of His own Being:
By the grace of the Guru, made known to men.[16]

Do believers not all touch common ground here? Isn't it
presumptuous of us, out of the depths of our ignorant
complacency, to call such visionaries heathens?

Today so much superfluous baggage adheres to the idea
of God that the word has become either alienating or
meaningless to many people. 'You say God is love, we say
love is God,' shrugs my Tibetan Buddhist friend, Tendzin
Choegyal, simplifying matters, 'so what's the difference?'
Didn't Simone Weil write that the only power God has is
that of moving us to show love to each other? All the major
religions would accept that that is so, however much they
may fail to put the ideal into practice. If you truly know
how to love, what do labels matter? They only serve to cloud
our perception of the truth. 'It seems to me, Govinda,' says
Hermann Hesse's Siddhartha, 'that love is the most important thing in the world. It may be important to great thinkers

to examine the world, to explain and despise it. But I think it is only important to love the world, not to despise it, not for us to hate each other, but to be able to regard the world and ourselves and all beings with love, admiration and respect.'[17]

Thursday 15 December 1994

Having acknowledged my debt to Eastern sacred writings, I must hasten to acknowledge an equal if not greater debt to a book by an Anglican theologian, William Vanstone. *Love's Endeavour, Love's Expense* is one of the most illuminating works I have ever read, a book to change lives. I was bowled over by it. And yet it almost passed me by. It had won the Collins Biennial Religious Book Award in 1979, two years before I myself became a judge on that particular panel. In the following years I had so many short-listed books to read that the last thing I wanted to do was spend time reading previous winners. It was relatively recently that Mary O'Hara asked me if I'd read it, and to forestall her inevitable demand that if I had not I should do so forthwith, I fibbed that I'd read it ages ago, when it first came out. However, my conscience nagged a bit, and one day I went guiltily out, bought the book and began to read.

Because *Love's Endeavour, Love's Expense* has become crucial to my understanding of what Frank and I are going through right now, I want to try and set down, however inadequately, what Vanstone says. He begins by talking about human love. If we want to arrive at a definition of true human love, he says, we can only do so by saying categorically (from hard-won, usually painful experience) what it is not: a) it is not limited or conditional; b) it does not manipulate or control; and c) it is committed and involved. Authentic human love, therefore, is a) limitless; b) precarious; and c) vulnerable. Now the logic of this for Christians, who say that God is love, is that without these three characteristics God's love could not be authentic. It must be limitless, it must be risk-taking and it must be vulnerable; *not* all-powerful, judgmental, controlling; but self-emptying, risky and vulnerable.

For me, that is a blinding insight. It means first that the loving activity of the ultimate ground of our being is poured out unceasingly and unreservedly on the whole universe; on that material creation which is coming to birth at every second, every hour, every day, and of which we human beings are the cutting edge, with the power to make or mar.

Second, it implies that this boundless love does not control or manipulate or in any way 'use' its object. It operates in unknown territory. It always runs the risk of being rejected. Rejection is all too frequent, and we give this destructive refusal of love the name of 'evil'. But redemption is also part of this loving creative process, since the possibility of turning evil to good is always there. 'That which is created is "other" than He who creates,' writes Vanstone. 'Its possibility is not fore-known but must be discovered . . . worked out in the creative process itself; and . . . the working-out must include the correction of the step which has proved a false step, the redemption of the move which, unredeemed, would be tragedy.'

This understanding of evil as always containing the possibility of its own redemption by grace rules out the repellent idea that God visits evil on us for some inscrutable purposes of his own. On the contrary, his will is that *we* ourselves should make good the world's mistakes and thus turn tragedy into triumph. We and we alone are the instruments of creation; but we so often fail to hear or understand the still, small voice of conscience which tells us so. Vanstone again:

> To interpret the creation as the work of love is to interpret it as the new, as the coming-to-be of the hitherto unknown, and so as that for which there can be no precedent and no programme. If the creation is the work of love, its 'security' lies not in its conformity to some pre-determined plan but in the unsparing love which will not abandon a single fragment of it, and man's assurance must be *the assurance not that all that happens is determined by God's plan, but that all that happens is encompassed by His love.*[18]

(The italics are mine. I find that assertion deeply compelling.)

Third, this love is vulnerable, not in the sense that it can be in any way diminished or destroyed, but because there is never any certainty that it will be accepted. God's helplessness waits on our good will. The power to accept or reject has passed to us; our response is of paramount importance, for we are the ones responsible for the triumph or tragedy of creation. And the tragic possibility (all too often fulfilled) is that the love may have been offered in vain. We reject the challenge of love, and selfishness triumphs, bringing a trail of destruction in its wake. Until the moment, that is, when someone finds in him or herself 'the power of yet further endeavour to win back and redeem that which was going astray'.

There have been many 'someones' like that in the history of the world. Avatars, the Hindus call them – the Godhead finding expression in human form to show an endangered humanity the way back to sanity. Gautama the Buddha was certainly one such, St Francis of Assisi another, to mention but two. We dare to hope there may be one or two around today to rescue us from the cesspit we have dug for ourselves. (Our century has already been blessed by Gandhi and Martin Luther King, but their message has gone largely unheeded.) For Christians, of course, the incarnate once-for-all expression of that 'someone' is Jesus of Nazareth who by his unselfish, self-emptying love showed human beings the way to become what they were meant to become, the way to become fully human. Calvary represents both the inevitable tragedy which follows the rejection of love's way, and the triumph of its final redemption.

In a letter to me, my friend Jessica once summed up our redemptive role in creation so memorably that I put it straight into my anthology:

> Each moment, each happening, each mental state, good or bad, is a starting-point for God's creative power. It helps if we actually will it to be so, if we open our hearts in prayer, tuning in to God, recognising that everything in life is his and that all things have a purpose. The emptiness, the dryness, the darkness may all be understood then as a fresh beginning in which we glimpse the truth of the human destiny, that all is a gift, that we are loved, that in having nothing we possess all things. The mercy of God underpins us and nothing, no matter how dreadful, can take away that mercy and love.

All these insights are to be treasured. I must not lose sight of them in the difficult weeks that lie ahead.

Sunday 18 December 1994

Frank rang nurse Madeleine this afternoon to ask what could be done if he suddenly found himself unable to get up at all. I think he wants to make sure she has thought about the possibilities, though I don't know how he could doubt it. We have now discussed having a bed downstairs by the patio doors. Events are moving fast. As I overheard him say to his friend Gerard on the phone, 'The secondaries are unfortunately rapidly overtaking the primaries.'

The days go by, the year draws to its close and death comes ever nearer. Last night I was appalled to see how swollen Frank's right foot and ankle were. The elastic of the sock was cutting into his leg. I had to hunt around for socks with looser tops.

This morning he tried to get to the shower. Afterwards I found him in a crumpled heap on the bed. The short distance from bed to shower cubicle had proved too much – and he knew he would never again make the attempt. He was lying there, looking helplessly at the sock in his hand, unsure what to do with it. I put it on for him and he was too weary to protest.

Wilfred Wilson Gibson's poem, *Lament*, buzzed insistently round in my head,

A bird among the rain-wet lilac sings –
But we, how shall we turn to little things
And listen to the birds and winds and streams
Made holy by their dreams,
Nor feel the heartbreak at the heart of things?

How indeed to live normally? The world does feel a comfortless place to be in – everyone with their own share of that heartbreak at the heart of things. Shirley du Boulay has just rung to say that our old friend Peter Hebblethwaite has just died. Hard to take it in, since I'd had a chatty letter from him only last week, full of plans for a new book. He had been ill in November, he wrote, but the crisis had passed.

Then earlier today his heart suddenly gave out. Poor Margaret, I must write to her.

Yet good things do happen – like having Kit, our Oxford Aunt, looking after us this past week. A lively, extrovert personality, very cheering to have around, and an excellent cook. Unfortunately, my eye operation has not been an unqualified success, since I showed an allergic reaction either to the stitch material or to the eye-drops I was given. (The latter have now been changed.) I still have to wear dark glasses and can neither read or write, except in a near-blind sort of way. My main worry is whether this will affect my capacity to look after Frank. Kit leaves us tomorrow, I'm sorry to say. I don't know what we'd have done without her – or, *help*, what we *will* do without her!

Monday 19 December 1994

Frank feels quite well now as long as he's in bed. He can even convince himself he's OK really, until he starts to try and get up. He underwent the usual calvary this morning, getting himself up and dressed and somehow dragging himself downstairs. He departed in the taxi for Charing Cross Hospital, but mechanically now, with nothing left to hope for. Madeleine rang shortly after he left. She has spoken to Raoul who will be seeing Frank later this week, when the course of treatment ends. She says the next thing will be palliative care. It's all that's left – making him as comfortable as possible while waiting for the end.

When pressed, she told me what Raoul had said, that the meningeal area of the spine was affected by the cancer, and that this accounted for everything – the backache, the neuropathy, the appalling constipation, the sluggish waterworks, and the depression. I asked her how we could deal with the last of these at least, given that Frank has never before in his life admitted to being depressed. I know he's terribly agitated about how I'm going to cope when he's gone, so I just don't think he'll pour out his fears to me. He's been protecting me all through our life together – probably by today's standards over-protecting – and it's too late for him to stop now.

Madeleine won't hazard a guess about his life-expectancy. Even now, she says, the cancer could go into remission, in which case it would be neither better nor worse, just static. But she did say, very gently, that she did not think he would see another Christmas after this one. I knew that, of course, but how I hated to hear it spelled out! Frank's on an upswing again. A duty nurse at Charing Cross told him this morning that sometimes you don't see any results till a week or two after the end of the treatment. She meant well, I'm sure, and the fragile hope she offered seems to have cheered him up, so I'll have to play along with it. But I dread his next appointment in January when he will inevitably discover that nothing has changed.

Our friends are so very supportive; we shall never be out of their debt. The cards and letters still pour in, bringing with them their assurance of affection.

Tuesday 20 December 1994

Frank came back from Charing Cross down-hearted, no longer quite so confident about what the nurse told him. But he rallied later. Nick has another ear infection and is miserable in his silent world. When Nick is ill, I feel more than ever helpless.

One bit of good news: a Christmas card from David and Christine Winter announces their imminent removal to Newbury. David was for many years my producer on BBC Radio 4's *Sunday*, a friend and counsellor as well as one of the wittiest and most entertaining companions I have ever known. (The gentle giant, Gerald Priestland, was another one.)

A strange thing once happened. It was in November 1972, when David had asked me to write the scripts for five documentary programmes on Radio 4's *Forty Years of Religious Broadcasting*. Suddenly I was told that my mother had suffered a coronary and was in hospital. Frank and I rushed up to St Helens to be with her when she died. On the morning of her death, after I left the hospital, I was sitting in an armchair in her house, knowing that I had to go through her things and put the house on the market before returning to London. There was a gilt tea trolley near me with letters on it, and I pulled it towards me, thinking to start in a small way by sorting her correspondence. As I picked up a pile of letters, the tears began to flow. My mother had looked so very dead, and it was hard to believe in any sort of life after death. Then, realising I was about to drench the letters in my hand with tears, I shook my head and turned my attention to them. To my surprise – and it still amazes me when I recall the moment – what I held in my hand was not a pile of letters at all, but a book, *Hereafter: Is There a Life After Death?* by David Winter. I hadn't even known he had written it. My aunt Betty, who had lived with my mother, had not seen the book before and was puzzled to see it now. We both knew that, devout Catholic though she was, my mother had had an absolute horror of death and the subject was tabu in front of her. As far as we knew, she had had no premonition of approaching death, so it seemed unlikely that she had broken with precedent and begun to read a book on the subject. Yet there was the book in my hands, written by one of my closest friends, someone to whom I might have turned to for sympathy had I been at home. It was uncanny to say the least, and I still find it somewhat shivery.

Very touching letters this morning. Basia and Robin Kemball write from Switzerland, with prayers 'for even more faith and courage than you already have'. (Alas, I seem to have very little of either.) Others assure us that we're in their prayers every hour of every day, and one of my childhood friends feels guilty because he should somehow 'have known what was happening without being told'. There was a beautiful card from Ireland. I didn't recognise the name, but as it's from Dun Laoghaire, maybe it's a friend of Mary O'Hara's. Whoever it was enclosed a poem called 'In Secret'.

Come in,
    and close the door.
My heart knows things
    the mind can never reach
Knows that darkness can be
    light.
Knows that absence hides
    the presence.
Knows that not knowing
    is the way to wisdom.

Come in, my soul,
    abide.
And I will speak
    without words,
Into the stillness

that clamours all around.
I will be held by Him
    whom I can never touch.
And hear the language
    I have never learned
    but understand.

Receiving, I shall give,
    And without doing
    be at peace
In this secret centre of
    my heart's home.

See how the darkness glows
and how the silence rings.

The poem was signed M. M. C. and I still don't know who
that is.

A strange day. At one time there were as many as six
people round Frank's bed. He seemed exhilarated and not
at all tired. But tomorrow is the last radiotherapy session.
Then, what?

Thursday 22 December 1994

Raoul met Frank with the words, 'It seems you have us
beat, Frank', but has asked to see him again in January, in
case the radiotherapy takes belated effect. I expected Frank
to come home depressed, but he seemed relatively cheerful,
despite being sad to say goodbye to Steven, the driver who
has taken him to Charing Cross every day and to whom he
has become quite attached. Every day Steven found a
wheelchair for him, pushed him up to the ward, waited for

him. He was so considerate and kind that the nurses all thought he was Frank's son.

Frank astounded me this evening by saying that he didn't think his condition was terminal. Being bedridden seems to be his worst case scenario. I know he's deluding himself, but now isn't the time to say so. He complained of pains in his head last night, and today I feel sure he's had a mini-stroke. His speech was a bit slurred; he was repeating himself, getting names confused, asking questions he'd just had answered.

Friday 23 December 1994

A bad night again. He had acute shooting pains in his ankles every few seconds for several hours. We called the doctor, and it was Colin who came. When I told him that Frank does not think his condition is terminal, he assured me that Frank was putting on an act to protect me. I don't think that's so, but in any case we mustn't disabuse him – he's got to be left with whatever hope he needs. Later on will be time enough to discuss death. Colin is sure it's only a matter of time now. He agrees about the mini-stroke and thinks that the cancer may well be affecting his brain. But he is still confident that all pain and discomfort can be dealt with.

Our friend Trevor, the Anglican curate, had arrived meanwhile and had been having coffee with Frank. Frank confided that until last week he had been hopeful that he would get better, but that suddenly in a blinding flash he'd recognised that he would not. But Trevor agrees that he's steeling himself to being bedridden, rather than to actually dying.

More visitors – Anne and Mike with some wine; the physio with elastic stockings to keep down the swellings in his ankles; Jenny, the nurse, with some tubigrip; and Sue with the trousers that had had to be exchanged at M&S. (Frank has decided that women's slacks with elastic waists might be easier for him to put on than men's trousers now, so we've been experimenting.) Everyone commented on how tired I looked. I *am* tired, but also my eyes continue to be sore and I have one of those colds that refuse to go away.

Poor Frank, I'm so unutterably sad for him. Getting from his chair to his desk or, worse, struggling from his chair to the loo, knocks all the stuffing out of him. And I'm more and more sure about that mini-stroke. His writing is becoming alarmingly spindly and illegible.

Later

He was dead tired tonight and went up to bed about 8 p.m. Before supper, he put his head in his hands and asked, 'Is this ever going to end? Ever?' His decline has been so rapid. Even when we first came to this house six weeks ago, he was still walking – with one stick. Shortly before we left the old house, he had driven us both to the surgery for a flu jab. But one day soon after we moved in, he got the car out of the garage, then stopped and looked at me miserably. 'I can't do it,' he said. 'I'll never be able to drive again.' It was another of those irreversible moments. Today we've gone way past the mere inability to drive. Now I wonder if he'll ever to be able to stand again.

Boxing Day 1994

We thought we might manage to enjoy Christmas in spite of everything, but we were both hung over by the knowledge that it was our last. Because of my eye condition, and the fact that I am still pretty helpless, Ginny, a generous neighbour who's in the catering business, offered to part-cook our Christmas dinner at her house and finish it off at ours. It was a relief to know that that was being taken care of but I felt very fragile. Vincent – one of the eucharistic ministers from church – brought Frank Holy Communion at 9.30 a.m., then drove me to the 10 a.m. Mass. When people began asking me how Frank was I burst into tears, and at Communion time I very nearly blubbed into the chalice.

Frank enjoyed all his presents. But he didn't get up till 11 a.m., was back in bed by 3 p.m. and asleep by 10 p.m.

This year I hadn't felt at all inclined to put up Christmas decorations. Kit made a few twig arrangements before she left and started to string the cards up on ribbons. I've gone on doing that, but nothing else. I can't just leave the cards lying about; there are far too many of them. The last ones have been strung up on their ribbons today, and I rather hope that no more will arrive as I've run out of ribbon. Delia sent a picture of the Christ Child being offered out of the burning bush to Moses, representing the human race. Bill Naylor, my cousin-by-marriage, wrote, 'It is the deep sorrow and feeling of helplessness which is almost overwhelming. I wish I could just hold your hands. All love and hopes. Bill'.

Thursday 29 December 1994

Frank is trying to wean himself off the steroids, and the awful breathlessness has returned. He is more or less permanently tired now, and is spending as much time in bed as out of it. This morning he tried to get up, struggled into his shirt, then flopped back on the bed, worn out by the effort. He stayed in bed for the rest of the morning, without the energy even to read or listen to the radio; his only visitor being Mr Munn, the hearing-aid specialist, who adjusted his aid and took the spare one away for repair. Frank asked him about a noise he'd heard in his left ear just before he went completely deaf in that ear. Mr Munn confirmed that the noise was a sign of the hearing packing up. Frank told me about it. 'It was just like a bell tolling,' he said. 'Significant, really. A bell tolling for one about to die.' So he does know.

Friday 30 December 1994

He felt really well this morning – while in bed. But when he tried to get up, it was a different story. He persisted, however, and was downstairs by 11.30 a.m. to see the chiropodist. As the stair-lift touched base he had a coughing fit, and coughed up sputum flecked with blood. When the chiropodist had gone, he admitted that the same thing had happened on Christmas morning, but he hadn't wanted to frighten me. It was disturbing, and neither of us knew what to make of it. But Frank's thoughts were obviously turning in the direction of death, and when I next went in the room, he said with a great rush of emotion (and he has never been an emotional man), 'I'd like to buy you a ring.' It was too much. I honked and ran out of the room. Later, when I had pulled myself together, we pored through the jewellery section of the Argos catalogue. The ring will have to come from Argos – otherwise we wouldn't be able to choose it together, and that is the whole point.

Nick has been incredibly helpful today. He took his shopping bag and went to the corner shop to get various basics that we needed, then returned on his own initiative because we were out of cereal for Mark and the children who are arriving this evening. I showed him how to get the loft ladder down and he climbed up to find the cot and pass the various sections down to me. He was very pleased with himself. After lunch, I suggested, without too much optimism, that maybe he'd like to hoover the carpet. He was so carried away that he vacuumed the whole house. Somehow I don't think he'll repeat the performance in a hurry. But it was good while it lasted!

Monday 2 January 1995

How I had dreaded New Year! For once there can be no doubt of what it will bring. It will be our last together. Mark and Trish (seven months pregnant with their third child) arrived on New Year's Eve with Timothy and Danielle. Nick, who generally prefers to stay up in his own room to watch TV, announced that he would come downstairs for 'Auld Lang Syne'. Frank spent most of the evening in bed, but came down on the stair-lift at 10.30 p.m. Though none of us felt like celebrating, we switched on the Clive James programme on BBC 1, and just before midnight Mark dutifully went outside with his piece of bread and a £1 coin. When I let him in on the stroke of midnight, we hugged each other hard, the words 'Happy New Year' nearly strangling us both. 'Auld Lang Syne' was the ordeal we had all known it would be. We joined hands with Frank who was propped up on foam cushions in his specially raised chair – and we all did our damnedest to sing. It came out more like croaking. Nick enjoyed himself hugely, though – he was the only one with dry eyes.

Went by taxi to Guildford to see Frank's twin Maureen and her husband Peter. They have been so anxious for Frank to see their new conservatory, yet none of us was sure he'd be able to make it. He made a Herculean effort and the day turned out well, despite its sad overtones. Peter had even built up a ramp outside the front door for the wheelchair. Frank was delighted to be there and seemed quite like his old self – Maureen and Peter have always brought out the best in him. We had lunch, then they drove us back home and stayed overnight. Frank was so exhilarated he didn't show any sign of tiredness – until it suddenly overpowered him.

Next day he was completely pole-axed.

Trevor, who took me down to the optician's this afternoon, was raving about another book by William Vanstone called *The Stature of Waiting*. As he talked about it, I realised that Mary has also been enthusing about it, but I'd been too tired to notice. It can't possibly be as good as *Love's Endeavour, Love's Expense*. Or can it? I must get Mary to lend it to me, so that I can read it when I get my sight back. For the moment I have to settle for audiobooks, but, apart from the Alan Bennett diaries, they all send me to sleep by the middle of side one. I yearn for the printed page.

Monday 9 January 1995

Frank said today that much of the time he feels he's some-where else. He's certainly getting more and more exhausted for more of the time. Yesterday, Barbara and Francis Minter came over from Banbury and it was 2.30 p.m. before he could summon the energy to get up and join us downstairs for lunch. (Thank heavens for that stair-lift. We couldn't possibly have managed without it.) Today he's terribly tired and confused. He said somewhat bitterly that we'd missed out on the quality time we'd been 'promised' at the beginning. 'You and Mary must make the most of this quality time,' Madeleine had said in August, but if quality time had come our way, we certainly hadn't noticed.

Tendzin Choegyal phoned this afternoon. 'Only God is real, Mary, remember that,' said the disembodied voice coming over the ether from India. No sooner had I put the phone down than Peter Maynard rang from Quito to assure us of his and Maruja's love and prayers. And Karen from LA. Such welcome moral support from all over the world.

Tuesday 10 January 1995

Full house for most of the day. Frank was pretty well comatose but a visit from Anne made him perk up. She is very good with him, and he's helping her too.

In the afternoon, the occupational therapist called to discuss elastic stockings and modular 'Bath Bubbles'. Frank was dismayed to find that with the Bubble he'd still have to swing his legs into the bath, which would, of course, be impossible. So he's settled for a stool strategically placed in the shower. Less exciting, but safer. Madeleine and Jenny arrived meanwhile and decided to order a new, streamlined zimmer frame on wheels for him. (He has to lift the present one off the ground as he walks and the effort is virtually beyond him.) Madeleine unfortunately depressed him by saying that the exhaustion was almost certainly caused by the cancer and was not just a side-effect of all the drugs he is taking. He didn't really want to hear that – it underlines the speed with which the cancer seems to be taking over his life.

There was an interesting *Blessings* letter today – I still intermittently get mail from all over the world about the book. It came from Myanmar, which I think is the new name for Burma. The writer of the letter and her husband were given a copy of *Blessings* some years ago 'and read it together quite a few times, always finishing up by realising how blessed we both were in so many ways'. But the woman's husband died earlier this year and the bereavement was painful. As her sight is poor (she's blind in one eye, with a cataract on the other), she asked her sister-in-law to read *Blessings* to her yet again. She seems to find endless comfort in it. 'I have particularly related to what you wrote about suffering,' she says, 'and I find it is possible to forget oneself and to see and enter into the lives of others. So thank you so much for showing me the way to turn suffering into compassion. This – and finding that God's grace is sufficient for every step of the way are helping me so much in the planning of a new life. Yours gratefully, R. T.' Funny how sometimes these letters arrive at the moment when they're most needed. I must write and thank her for reminding me of what is important.

Wednesday 11 January 1995

Frank is sleeping most of the time now. The occupational therapist came in with a load of gadgets: a bath-seat that moves up and down – but terribly large and cumbersome; a shower-stool; a gadget for pulling the elastic stockings on with – only it seems more complicated than doing it the usual way; a pronged stick for picking things up off the floor. (What a lot of prepositions that sentence has!) We both felt wearied by the sheer volume of all these goodies, though it has to be said that Frank is over the moon about his new

zimmer on wheels. It makes a big difference. He almost
zips around with it. Well, almost.

Thursday 19 January 1995

Nick's thirtieth birthday. We have had an absolute flood of
visitors – all of them helpful and very welcome. But the
constant running up and down stairs, answering doors and
telephones, making tea and coffee, is getting to me. After
one visitor had departed this morning, I found myself on
the edge of hysteria. When I went upstairs for Frank's
breakfast tray, I found that his hearing-aid battery had
packed up and he couldn't hear me. I went down to look
for a replacement but couldn't find one. My frustration
boiled over. I stormed at Frank for not checking on his
batteries, when hearing is so vital to him. I knew I was
overwrought and was being unfair, but I simply couldn't
help myself. It was like the lid coming off a pressure cooker.
He looked at me sadly and said, 'You don't understand. I
know what I should do, but I just don't have any energy.' I
felt ashamed, but was still shaking with hysteria when
Johnny arrived at 10.15 a.m. I left him with Frank and went
downstairs to take a beta-blocker, one of those that Lilian
had given me to ward off panic attacks. But I was too far
gone and just got more and more emotional. I knew I needed
the release of tears, but dared not cry because two friends
from Maidenhead were coming to see me on their way to
have lunch somewhere nearby. The inevitable happened –
the welcoming smile with which I greeted them was replaced
by a storm of tears before they'd even got beyond the door.

After that I felt better – except that I was full of remorse
for having shouted at Frank when he was lying there
helpless. I went in to say sorry, but he was fast asleep. I

73

apologised later, and of course everything was all right. He understands the pressure I'm under. But he was feeling ghastly himself and said gloomily, 'It's a pretty poor outlook, isn't it? I seem to be getting worse every day.' I tried to point out that he had good days as well as bad, but he couldn't actually think of any and nor could I. In any case, he's right; the outlook is pretty bleak. Why pretend otherwise?

Madeleine came. She didn't find it surprising that I had cracked up this morning, but I'm determined not to let it happen again. She thinks that Frank will remain in control of his faculties till the end, and that he will just fade away gently. When she went up to see him, he asked her point-blank how much longer she thought he had. He seemed resigned when she said, just single-figure months.

Sonia Perry arrived with two birthday cakes she had made for Nick; one in the shape of a three, the other a nought. He loved that, especially when I added a magic birthday candle that wouldn't blow out. He positively cackled with delight as he blew and blew and the flame rushed back. Thirty he may be, but mostly Nick is still a child. I did a special birthday dinner for him, some of his favourite dishes, and with his favourite people, Ellen and Tracey Maleham, as guests. Ellen and her daughter, Tracey, had come on the scene a few months after that other special person, my aunt Betty, had died, and they had almost immediately taken over Betty's central role in his life. He tells them things he tells no one else and proudly refers to them as '*my* people'. When he is with them he is totally happy, and no celebration is complete without them.

Suddenly I was overcome with sadness. I caught Frank's eye and knew the same thought was in both our minds: he would not be here to celebrate Nick's thirty-first birthday. Every event seems to be another 'last time'. Another final curtain ringing down.

Monday 23 January 1995

Today I was due to have the laser treatment for my eye, but unfortunately I developed conjunctivitis over the week-end. My eye has been extremely painful – and although Sue drove me to the hospital for the treatment, Mr Moss took one look at me and packed me off home with instructions to return next week.

Trevor sat with Frank this afternoon. He told me afterwards that without prompting Frank had brought up the subject of the funeral, saying that he wanted no fuss, just a simple requiem at the Catholic church, followed by interment in the local churchyard. Later on, Frank confessed to me that he was reading *The Times* obituaries every day now and had been discouraged to note that the average age is much higher than his own sixty-seven. He was beginning to feel it was a bit unfair. But we talked it over, and agreed that we have both had a reasonable lifespan and cannot complain. I suppose it's natural for us to feel resentful when death's shadow begins to fall – we're never really ready to let go of life.

Monday 30 January 1995

I'm realising just how easy it is to let things get one down. It's the small things you have to watch. Perhaps it's because I'm permanently confined to the house but last week, in spite of all my good intentions, I found myself getting infuriated by the chaos in our bedroom. It's not a large room, anyway, and we were a bit pushed for space right from the start, but now the mess seems to have taken on a life of its own. Frank spends most of his time up there and every morning and afternoon I set out on the bed: newspapers, telephone, directories general and personal, organiser, writing block, papers, envelopes, stamps, correspondence, pens, documents of all kinds, etc. etc. After he gets up and again at night I have to stow all these things away somehow. I know it's unimportant but I find myself getting irritated and behaving as though somehow Frank should be able to manage these things for himself – which he manifestly can't. I'll have to stop being so irrational. What does a bit of chaos matter?

To calm myself I wandered into the study and picked a book from the shelves. It was *A Guide to the Bodhisattva's Way of Life* which Tendzin Choegyal's son, Lodoe, had given me a couple of years earlier in Dharamsala. 'An exchange of western and eastern ideas,' this remarkable sixteen-year-old had written on the flyleaf, 'in the search for the true meaning of life.' I remembered Lodoe pointing out his favourite verse:

> Whatever joy there is in this world
> All comes from desiring others to be happy,
> And whatever suffering there is in this world
> All comes from desiring myself to be happy.

I opened the book at random and peered at the words short-sightedly.

> There is nothing whatsoever
> That is not made easier through acquaintance,
> So through becoming acquainted with small harms
> I should learn to patiently accept greater harms.

And

> I should not be impatient

With heat and cold, wind and rain,
Sickness, bondage and beatings;
For if I am, the harm they cause me will increase.[19]

So, for heaven's sake, ignore the mess upstairs. It's a small price to pay for Frank's life being made more tolerable.

Tuesday 7 February 1995

I have now had the magical laser treatment and my sight has returned to normal at last. It's fantastic. I was beginning to think I should never see properly again.

All last week I kidded myself that Frank's condition had begun to stabilise. He seemed to have reached a plateau – perhaps the half-hoped-for remission. Today I'm less sure. He slept virtually all day until 5 p.m., then got up and came down on the stair-lift at 6.30 p.m. But by 9.30 p.m. he was feeling breathless, was short of oxygen, and had pains everywhere. I begged him to ring Madeleine, but he insisted on hanging on till morning.

Hanging on. Waiting. It's what our lives largely consist of now. I've been thinking a lot about the book that Trevor was so enthusiastic about, and that Mary O'Hara brought for me last week, Vanstone's *The Stature of Waiting*.[20] Vanstone makes the point that we in the West attribute worth to ourselves and each other only when we are doing, succeeding, achieving, rising to challenges. But there comes a time in everyone's life when we move from the active to the passive, being-done-to mode. At times of rejection, disappointment, unemployment, sickness and failure we often have no choice but to accept passively. Jesus, for example, from the moment he was 'handed over' to the authorities in the garden of Gethsemane, passed from the active to the passive mode – his 'passion' – forced from then on to be at the receiving end of anything people might choose to do to him. This to us is failure, the negation of whatever meaning we attribute to ourselves. And failure is the one unforgivable sin in today's world. But Vanstone argues (as did Teilhard de Chardin) that these times of passive waiting are the times of growth, when we become catalysts for the spiritual growth of others as well as ourselves. When we accept to 'be-done-to' we grow rather than diminish in stature.

I saw the truth of that in my aunt Betty before she died. Betty came to live with us in 1972 after the death of my mother. She was immensely active and energetic, and the fact that we needed her was crucial to her happiness. But when – about 1979 when she was in her mid-eighties – she was no longer capable of being active, she was convinced she was nothing but a useless old woman. With her self-image in ruins, she lost her bearings. She refused to accept a passive role, would not allow us to help her, and insisted on attempting activities which were obviously impossible for her. Betty, always the most selfless and unassuming of people, began to see Frank and me (especially me) as a threat, and for a year or two the tensions built up to an almost intolerable level. We were all miserable. But in the last few weeks of her life, she suddenly 'let go', stopped struggling, allowed us to look after her, relaxed – and became immeasurably happier. It was a kind of miracle. Those last few weeks of Betty's life seem in retrospect to have been touched by grace. They were a time for mending fences and rediscovering our deep affection for each other.

And now I am seeing the same process at work in Frank, who all his life has been in control, in the driving seat, able to confront any problem and see it off. He too is now having to accept a passive role, and in the process is being transformed into a gentler, more loving person. Shirley du Boulay, who came to lunch on Sunday, was struck by his courage and dignity and by a new warmth in him. Anne has just this morning said that knowing Frank at this period of his life has been a revelation to her, has made her appreciate what is really important in life, and made her see the value of simple, undemanding goodness.

I'm beginning to understand that spiritual growth is much simpler than we imagine. Frank, I know, has never given much thought to spiritual matters; he's not that way inclined. He's always been the practical one, never agonising over the great philosophical 'why' questions of life, concerned only with the more pragmatic 'how'. He has never been prone to self-doubt and has accepted himself without question. But, however one defines it, he *is* showing signs of spiritual growth and everybody who comes into contact with him notices it. 'The stature of waiting'. When Fr Seamus came to see us last week, I talked to him about Frank's continuing lack of interest in the eternal verities, even now when he is about to die. Personally, I don't think it matters. He is a good man, he has a kind of faith and it's too late for him to change, anyway. Seamus agrees, saying that simple goodness and a mind at peace with itself are all we need at the end.

Wednesday 8 February 1995

He is more alert this morning, and is tackling some correspondence in bed. I myself woke up feeling strangely happy. I tried to analyse the feeling, and decided that it stemmed from being where I ought to be and doing (more or less) what I have to do. Being the right person in the right place at the right time. Then I came downstairs and found a letter from Shirley, saying how she had been struck by the fact that we were both so calm and 'just *being*, in so peaceful and receptive a way'. She is working on a biography of Bede Griffiths and has just been studying some of his correspondence at the Bodleian. She writes:

> I have just come across a line which reminded me of our conversation yesterday. 'The whole art of spiritual living is to want to do what we ought to do.' Don't you think that's splendid? And presumably it follows that to do what you *don't* want to do isn't necessarily virtuous. I'm always worried about the pious Christian who thinks it's better to do the things you don't want to do.

Shirley's letter echoed my own thoughts just a few minutes earlier – about the peace which comes from truly accepting the circumstances in which we find ourselves. Zen Buddhism claims we are obsessed with looking for God in the 'far-off', whereas we should be looking close at hand. (I have a rather good definition of Zen in my personal anthology. 'For Zen, the endpoint of man's journey is not "union with God". Zen insists that there has never been a separation. All that is needed is the flash of insight that makes one *see* it!'[21]) The only Zen story which I can ever remember springs to mind:

Novice: Master, teach me how to attain spiritual wisdom.
Master: Have you had your breakfast?
Novice (puzzled): Yes, but . . .
Master: Well, then, go and wash the dishes.

Thomas Merton once wrote that where we are now is where we have to be. The problems of the here and now are what we have to wrestle with. Dag Hammarskjøld wrote in *Markings*: 'What must come to pass should come to pass.

Within the limits of that "must", therefore, you are invulnerable.'[22] 'Life with all its gifts is essentially organic,' as Dennis Potter had told me in that Radio 4 interview, 'continually renewing itself, changing its face, moving from light to darkness; and we must accept to go with it, absorbing its changes, facing its choices, letting go . . .' As he spoke, he was – as ever – in great pain from his crippling arthropathy. All we have to do is let go, let ourselves *be*.

A card from David Winter announces that he and Christine have now moved to Newbury and want to come and see us. Funny, but amid all the happy memories of working with David at Broadcasting House, the memory that stands out most clearly is the address he gave at the funeral of our colleague and mutual friend, the Anglican priest, Robert Foxcroft. I can hear him now, recalling Robert's love of the Eucharist and adding: 'But we must never forget that the Eucharist is bread that has been broken and wine that has been poured out.' It sent shivers down my spine at the time, as, *a fortiori*, it does today. David presumes (correctly) that I no longer have time or opportunity for writing, and quotes the blind Milton in sympathy: 'And that one talent which is death to hide/lodg'd with me useless'. I was more than halfway through my fascinating research on the Dalai Lama and his family when Frank's illness struck. The book has obviously had to be put on the back burner since I have neither time nor energy nor enthusiasm at present for the work. This journal is probably a sort of surrogate book.

Friday 10 February 1995

Maureen and Peter have started coming each week for an overnight stay. Today Maureen left in tears. Perhaps, it's worse for her, his twin, than for anyone. Frank has been part of her life since they were born, and they have always been close. Both she and Peter find it very distressing to see him as he is now.

Margaret Hebblethwaite has an article about bereavement – 'The Widow's Tale' – in this week's *Tablet*. My first thought was that it was a bit premature – Peter has been dead for less than two months. How can she write about an experience which is still so new? But Margaret does tend to go for the big, dramatic gesture, and it is in fact a very good article about the early experience of widowhood. (What an ugly word widowhood is!) She's one step ahead of me in this area, though she's a quarter of a century younger. She speaks of the 'heightened experience, of peaks, of colour, of gratitude and the release of laughter as well as the anguish of tears at what now will never be'. Such conflicting emotions, as she copes with all the attention, the phone calls, letters, flowers, obituary notices and offers of help which surround her. She claims that as yet she has experienced no bleakness, but that is not to say there will not be any. Still, Margaret is tough and a survivor. I was moved by her account of going with the children to see Peter's body (will I want to do that? I'm pretty certain I won't):

> It was an important visit, for we looked at the truth in the strength of our togetherness, and the closed coffin would now hold no terrors for us. The ends of his fingers were blue, but they were still his fingers, and the face was still his face, though he was not in it. I stuttered Bede Jarrett's prayers through my tears, phrase by phrase, *We seem to give them back to thee, O God, who gavest them to us . . . And life is eternal, and love is immortal, and death is only an horizon, and an horizon is nothing save the limit of our sight.* We stared in stunned, motionless silence for a long,

> long time. Then eventually we broke the mood, and spoke
> together in a more relaxed way about the sight before our
> eyes.

Some people found the article distasteful, but many wrote
to the editor that they had found comfort and a kind of
liberation in it.

I have kept meaning to fish out *Le Milieu Divin* and reread
what Teilhard had to say about 'the passivities of diminishment'.[23] It seemed to me, dimly remembering the book, that
he said much the same thing as Vanstone in his *Stature of
Waiting*. I was right: the points he makes are the same; that
becoming object rather than subject, dependent rather than
active, done-to rather than doing, are an essential part of
life and of growth. The forces of diminishment, says
Teilhard, gradually establish a mastery over the forces of
life and drag us, physically vanquished, to the ground. We
can only overcome death by finding God in it. I quote:

> [Death] is the sum and type of all the forces that diminish
> us, and against which we must fight, without being able
> to hope for a personal, direct and immediate victory. Now
> the great victory of the Creator and Redeemer, in the
> Christian vision, is to have transformed what is in itself a
> universal power of diminishment and extinction into an
> essentially life-giving factor. God must, in some way or
> other, make room for himself, hollowing us out and
> emptying us, if he is finally to penetrate into us. And in
> order to assimilate us in him, he must break the molecules
> of our being so as to re-cast and re-model us. The function
> of death is to provide the necessary entrance into our
> inmost selves. It will put us into the state organically
> needed if the divine fire is to descend upon us. And in
> that way its fatal power to decompose and dissolve will

be harnessed to the most sublime operations of life. What was by nature empty and void, a return to bits and pieces, can, in any human existence, become fullness and unity in God.

Teilhard speaks of death as 'communion through diminishment' and this section of the book ends with a magnificent prayer:

After having perceived you as he who is, 'a greater myself', grant, when my hour comes, that I may recognise you under the species of each alien or hostile force that seems bent on destroying or uprooting me. When the signs of age begin to mark my body (and still more when they touch my mind); when the ill that is to diminish me or carry me off strikes from without or is born within me; when the painful moment comes in which I suddenly awaken to the fact that I am ill or growing old; and above all at that last moment when I feel I am losing hold of myself and am absolutely passive within the hands of great unknown forces; in all those dark moments, O God, grant that . . . I may understand that it is you who is painfully parting the fibres of my being in order to penetrate to the very marrow of my substance and bear me away within yourself.

Saturday 11 February 1995

Frank felt very sick this morning. Lilian came round just in time to catch him heaving his heart out. She gave him an injection to make him sleep and stop the queasiness. So – is it a bug? or the beginning of another phase of the cancer? I suppose a lot will depend on how he is over the next day or so. He was unable to see any of his visitors today.

Frank marginally better but utterly limp. It looks as though he may never get out of bed again. However, he's recovered an appetite. While Lilian was here this morning he actually asked for a Shredded Wheat. She recommends giving him milky things, so later I made some cream of vegetable soup. The duty nurse came and gave him a bed-bath, after which he looked a lot fresher but was completely done-in.

Everyone is being wonderfully kind. Anthony rang up to see if I'd like him to come over, but I think I'll be able to manage.

I found that little book of prayers by Michael Hollings and Etta Gullick – *The One Who Listens*[24] I had once given it to my close friend John (Harriott) – inscribed 'for *celui qui écoute*' and Shirley had returned it to me after his death from a heart attack in December 1990. There are lots of helpful things in it, the one I like best at the moment being:

> O God, our only help in time of need, be close to me in my sorrow, in your mercy give me strength to keep going, and help me to trust you whatever happens. Into your loving hands I commend myself and Frank: give us peace and rest in you.

And another fairly similar one:

> Lord, the one I love is sick and in great pain; out of your compassion heal him and take away his pain. It breaks my heart to see him suffer; may I not share his pain if it is not your will that he be healed? Lord, let him know that you are with him; support and help him that he may come to know you more deeply as a result of his suffering. Lord, be our strength and support in this time of darkness and give us that deep peace which comes from trusting you.

This morning the postman delivered a small packet for me. Inside was a phial of perfume and a printed card saying, 'Who Loves You? Look in *The Times* Valentine pages.' It would never in a million years have occurred to me to look in them. I'd even forgotten it was Valentine's Day, although we had always, even at the worst times, sent each other a Valentine. I looked up first Craig, then Mary – and found 'Mary, I love you. Valentines are for ever. Frank'. I dissolved into a veritable gust of sobs from which it took me quite a long time to recover. It was so unexpected and poignant, and – quite heartbreaking.

He had a little breakfast. Anne came to drive me to Hungerford to have my hair done – she and Mike should have gone off to their place in Madeira yesterday, but they postponed their trip to be with Anne's mother who is also dying. She went up briefly to see Frank and give him a hug. 'Hurry back, both of you,' he said drowsily, already drifting off to sleep as we left. He slept most of today, in fact, despite the numerous visitors who came. Madeleine arrived with a new commode chair on wheels, a great improvement on the one we had before; Jenny came with an inflatable pressure mattress, a cage to keep the bedclothes off his feet, and a spray to counteract the dryness in his mouth. The social services are really magnificent.

Can it really have been less than a week ago that he was still coming down on the stair-lift to meals and staying to watch TV in the early evening? Nobody expected his health to lurch downhill with such devastating suddenness. It can be quite confusing at times, though. For part of each day he seems quite bright. Last night he spoke to both Anthony and Mark at some length on the telephone – a bit disjointed and rambling, but very chirpy. My friend Margaret (Griffiths) always says that when she rings and speaks to him, he laughs and jokes with her as he always did, and she finds it hard to realise that he's really very ill. She just has to take my word for it. Maureen and Peter came on Wednesday morning and there was a great deal of mutual teasing and laughter that evening. Yet when they left next morning, they were both distressed by the change in him.

Today he was too zonked to let Jenny give him a proper bed-bath, so she just gave him a light wash and rinsed out his mouth with a swab. Then he revived and asked for some breakfast, but when I took the tray up to him, he looked at it as though he didn't know what it was or what he was expected to do with it. When Lilian arrived and saw how he was, she said it seemed very unfair. She also said she presumed I still wanted to keep him at home. I assured her I did – if it's humanly possible. That's what we both want.

Lilian is now on the phone arranging for us to have nursing cover for the weekend. It's the measure of how seriously ill he is that a nurse will be coming in on both Saturday and Sunday. As I was expecting to have to go through the week-end on my own, I am mightily relieved.

Saturday 18 February 1995

We had a bad night – he was out of bed four times, which meant, each time, an hour-long struggle to move himself down the bed, on to the commode and then the whole procedure in reverse. It was terrible for him and each time I prayed he would not have to go through the ordeal again.

He's having great difficulty in passing water again, and there's been some talk of inserting a catheter. But he resists the idea strenuously because of his painful experience in August – was it really only August? – in the Oxford hospital.

The last time he got up was at 7 a.m., after which, thankfully, he slept till 11 a.m. When the duty nurse arrived, I went to get clean sheets and pyjamas out for her, but Frank was having none of it. He flatly refused to let her near to wash him. In the middle of this unexpected impasse, Colin West arrived to put a catheter in. Frank again refused. But as Colin persuaded him there was no real alternative, eventually he caved in. Unfortunately, it proved impossible to insert the catheter; the prostate gland was solid, said Colin. It's grown again since the prostatectomy in August and it's no wonder he's having such dreadful problems.

So here we have a big problem, and it seems likely that we're in for a number of nights like last night. It's an alarming prospect; the only good thing being that by morning Frank has no recollection of what happened – this morning he hotly denied to the nurse that he had been up at all in the night. He was actually quite indignant when I insisted that he had. In some ways I'm grateful for the fact that his mind has slipped a notch or two over the last few days. He seems to drift in and out of lucidity.

Sunday 19 February 1995

Last night was better, and he slept till 9.30 a.m. When I heard him stir, I went upstairs and found him trying to get out of bed to reach the grab-rail on the wall – and falling back again. I offered him in turn the water bottle, the bucket, a bowl, the commode, but he insisted that no, he would walk to the loo somehow. It cost him every ounce of strength, but he did it. Then, of course, he was unable to get off again. Fortunately Anthony was in the house and between us we wrestled him back to bed, where he promptly fell asleep.

Anthony had to go back home to Bristol, but felt I shouldn't be left alone to cope. He rang Mark, who said he would come over for the day with the family. Anthony went upstairs to say goodbye to Frank and came down struggling with tears, overwhelmed by the realisation that this time the goodbye might be for ever. He didn't know how to handle the possibility.

Frank again stubbornly refused to be washed. He told Terry, the nurse, he probably wouldn't see her or any of the other nurses again as very soon now he'd be up and walking around. Terry warned me to expect these erratic mood swings from now on.

He again asked for breakfast, and though he had ignored the first tray I tried again a second time. As I put the tray down, he asked me very politely if this was the same house he'd been in a week ago. I almost feel now that he only half knows who I am.

Mark, Trish and the children were still here when Seamus came to give Frank the Sacrament of the Sick – what we used to call the Last Rites. We all gathered round the bed. And as they reluctantly left for home, my old BBC friend, Frances Donnelly, now a best-selling novelist, arrived to stay with me for a few days.

We're entering the realm of *grand guignol*, grotesque waking nightmare. I struggled to get Frank on and off the commode, and nearly collapsed with the exertion. Then when I got him back into bed, I noticed all his bottles of pills lying empty on the quilt. He'd attempted to select the ones needed for night-time, putting them in the bottle I had specially marked 'night'. Unfortunately, instead of four tablets, he'd put about ten in the bottle, and they were all the wrong ones. I nearly had hysterics. I've now removed all the pills and put them where he won't be able to find them. Fortunately, I know exactly what tablets he is supposed to be taking and when. Until a few days ago I wouldn't have known, because until then he was capable of managing them himself. But now . . .

Monday 20 February 1995

A terrible night. Frank only tried to get up twice, but each time was unimaginably awful. It is now quite impossible for me to move him, he's a dead weight. In the morning I admitted defeat and arranged for a night nurse to come in tonight. Jenny came mid-morning, and she couldn't manage him on her own either. She had to ring for another nurse to come and help. Later, one of our oldest friends, Joe Cheetham, came for the day. In the afternoon the two of us managed to get him in and out of bed, but we were both pole-axed by the effort. It was a relief to know that I wouldn't have to cope alone during the night again: a night nurse would be arriving at 10 p.m.

The nurse, Dawn, was delightful. Nevertheless, when I left her and moved my things to the spare room where I was to sleep, I felt desperately sad. It was another final curtain ringing down – I knew that we would never again sleep in the same room.

Tuesday 21 February 1995

Dawn reported that Frank had slept till 4.30 a.m., before trying once again to get out of bed. She had given him diazepam last night but it had only been partially effective.

She got him back to bed, but he was attempting to get out again at 6.30 a.m. when she gave him his morning tablets. I saw her off at 7 a.m. and hoped against hope that Frank would stay asleep. Frances was still with me. At about 9.30 a.m. she heard him trying to get out of bed and shouted for me to come. I rushed upstairs. I'll draw a veil over the next half-hour, but it was undiluted hell. At the end of it I just broke down. The floodgates opened, and poor Frank was stroking my hair and asking me what the matter was. He really didn't have the faintest idea. That, at least, was a mercy.

Three nurses arrived soon after and stayed with him for about an hour, giving an enema, bathing him, changing the bedclothes. Frances went shopping for me, and as she left, Anne came and I broke down again on seeing her. Our neighbour Johnny arrived to see Frank and I took him upstairs. Frank seemed quite lucid for the most part, only wandering in his wits occasionally. But poor Johnny was very emotional when he came downstairs. He told me that although he had worked as a doctor in general practice for many years, this was the first time he'd ever watched a close friend die.

Frank had a bowl of soup, and asked for some fromage frais. I left it with him, and was surprised to hear Frances urgently calling again. He was half out of bed. I cajoled him back into it, just as I would have cajoled a small child – and he went straight back to sleep.

Had a long conversation with Anne about death. She is very upset about her mother who may die at any time. Why is it, she wondered, that we grieve so deeply over one person dying when we are well aware that death will happen to us all? I said that quite apart from the love that we have for that one special person, we suffer from our tragic inability to let go of them, our conviction that without that particular someone we will lose our sense of who we are. I believe the Buddhists are right to say that all suffering is caused by our desire for what we can't have, by our clinging to the past and refusing to accept the present. But I also believe that if we were able to detach ourselves from pain completely, we should be less than human. The suffering may be intolerable, but I think we have to accept to go through it, discovering our weakness and our humanity in its depths. We all pass this way at some time – suffering is the universal experience which binds us all, and through it we discover how much we need each other. Frank and I have drawn closer over this period than we have ever been in forty-two years of marriage (and six years of friendship before that), and undeniably there is a strange, fierce joy in the midst of all the pain. I remember Rosemary Foxcroft writing to say much the same thing after Robert had died. I've just looked up her letter: 'The horror and pain will always be with me,' she wrote, 'but also, I hope, the strength which Robert showed throughout the bad times. It was, I think, because of the great darkness that the shafts of light, when they came, were very bright and will last forever.'

I firmly believe that whatever or whoever God is, he or she or it shares the suffering with us. I do not and could not believe in a God who inflicts pain – like Ivan Karamazov, I would 'hand in my ticket'. 'Only a suffering God can help,' wrote Dietrich Bonhoeffer. Simone Weil believed that the cry of dereliction from the cross – My God, my God, why hast thou forsaken me? – was the cry of God entering into the suffering of all humanity. One of the most moving stories I have ever read came in Elie Wiesel's heart-rending book, *Night*. Forced to watch a Jewish boy die in prolonged agony on a gallows in Auschwitz,

'Where is God? Where is he?' a man behind me asked.

As the boy, after a long time, was still in agony on the rope, I heard the man crying again, 'Where is God now?' And I heard a voice within me answer, 'Here he is – he is hanging here on this gallows.'[25]

And in his novel, *Sophie's Choice*, William Styron makes a poignant comment on the incident. 'Auschwitz itself remains inexplicable,' he writes.

The most profound statement yet made about Auschwitz was not a statement at all but a response:
    The query: At Auschwitz, tell me, where was God?
    And the answer: Where was man?[26]

Colin came in before his afternoon surgery, and says that if Frank has not managed to pass water in twelve hours' time, he will send him to hospital for treatment. I agree, but don't want Frank to be frightened if they attempt to take him out of the house. (How on earth will they get him down the stairs?) Colin says they will sedate him.

The late afternoon was frightful. Seamus came to give him Communion, and was closely followed by Madeleine. By this time Frank was trying to get out of bed again and was in a very distressed state. Madeleine rolled up her sleeves and helped me manhandle him back. She then had to leave, but told me to call her at home if I needed her. I stayed with him, holding his hand, and about every ten minutes it was clear that he was in awful pain. 'Am I in a horror movie?' he asked, staring at me, bewildered. Things got worse and worse, so I telephoned through to the surgery with a message for Colin. By 7.45 p.m. I had got so desperate that I rang Madeleine, who came over instantly, bumping into Colin on the doorstep. They went upstairs to find that the bladder had now distended – and decided to get Frank into hospital without further delay. An ambulance was summoned. I cancelled the night nurse, rang Sue, packed an overnight bag and we were on our way within the hour. Sue and Desmond followed in their car in case I was to be brought back. What friends they are!

We waited on tenterhooks, but this time the fates had pity. The doctor at Basingstoke Hospital managed to insert a catheter, a long-term one which will last three months. Sadly, I think it will outlast Frank.

Wednesday 22 February 1995

Sue and Desmond brought me home at midnight, while Frank stayed overnight at the hospital. This morning, he was brought back by ambulance at 11.30 a.m., though I had been told not to expect him before the afternoon. He looked terribly ill as the men carried him in. I was furious with the ambulanceman who came in with his case. 'Doesn't talk much, your old man, does he?' he said. I could scarcely believe my ears, insensitivity not being something I associate with ambulancemen, for whom I have the highest regard.

The catheter is having its effect, thank God: Frank is no longer trying to get out of bed. Colin came, with the news that the blockage had been due partly to the prostate tumour and partly to the effect of the spinal cancer on the nerve-endings of the bladder. The registrar at the hospital had suggested transferring Frank to the orthopaedic department for further tests, but Colin thankfully had said no, he'd already suffered enough; far better for him to come home and enjoy what comfort he can in his last days.

Thursday 23 February 1995

It's unbelievable. He's a different person today, bright-eyed, smiling, cracking jokes. Maureen and Peter were here and his other sister, Kathleen, and her husband, David, came over from Cheam. I'll swear the latter thought I'd been exaggerating the reports of his illness. Sue came and sat with Frank while I took them all out for a bar-lunch. When we came back, he was still lively and cheerful. The difference is incredible, but of course it won't last. It's almost certain to be the big dipper syndrome again, unfortunately.

Jenny came with a back-up of two other nurses this morning. They suggest we get a hospital bed and install it downstairs. We'll have to move all the furniture around in the sitting-room, but it may be our only option.

Saturday 25 February 1995

Maureen and Peter stayed for three days, but now I'm on my own again and the house seems horribly quiet. I got an agency nurse in this morning, to wash Frank and change his sheets. Thursday's improvement was, inevitably, a flash in the pan. His mind has been wandering ever since. Yesterday morning he believed he was in a hotel and asked me if there were many other guests staying here. (Perhaps that's an understandable mistake; the house *has* seemed recently like a hotel.) He keeps on asking me if it's time to get up yet and when are we going home. This afternoon, when Anne's husband Mike came and sat with him for an hour, Frank started out by being quite lucid, then suddenly began talking rubbish. I find I can jolly him along for some of the time, but at others I just gag on the attempt. It's particularly painful when his eyes light up on seeing me, he squeezes my hand, or draws his fingers down the side of my face, saying, 'I love you.' 'I love you too,' I reply, but it's almost unbearable.

Vincent came with Communion. Frank looked pleased and actually said bits of the 'Our Father' with him, and made the sign of the cross. But Vincent was horrified at the change in him.

Later this evening he began to hallucinate about the telephone, which he said had been ringing non-stop. It hadn't. When Kathleen rang later, I answered the phone in the kitchen and suddenly realised Frank had picked up the extension in the bedroom, even though it had been put out of his reach. I heard his voice saying, 'Hello, Kathleen. Hang on, I'm just getting out of bed.' I was upstairs like a shot from a cannon. He was all right, still safely in bed, but under the impression that Kathleen was ringing for the sixth or seventh time that evening. Later on, Anthony rang and, though I'd again put the telephone out of reach, Frank must this time have struggled to reach it because I found him spread-eagled on the far side of the bed, half-off his own special mattress, with his face buried in the shaggy underblanket. (How I managed to haul him right way up I shall never know!) He again insisted that the phone had been ringing non-stop all evening – which was certainly not the case. There must be a ringing in his head. Has he now got tinnitus, on top of everything else?

Having had (at his own request) a small piece of chocolate, he was very sick. Fortunately I managed to get a bowl to him in time.

Sunday 26 February 1995

Poor Frank is being subjected to one physical indignity after another. In the kindest possible way, of course, but it's a chastening thought that most of us come to such ritual humiliation at the end. Fortunately I don't think he knows much about it.

Mark and Trish came today with the children. It was a dreadful ordeal for Mark, to go up and say goodbye to his father. He literally crumpled into a heap when he came downstairs. 'I'll never see him again,' he said, and wept unrestrainedly. After a while he had to pull himself together and get the two little ones ready for the drive back to Potters Bar, but he went on being terribly upset. Timmy kept saying, 'Don't cry, you two,' because, naturally, I wasn't exactly dry-eyed myself.

As soon as they had gone, I took Frank a slice of cake. He looked quite normal as he ate it, then asked in a friendly way, 'Do we know what time the trains are leaving?' 'What trains?' I asked. 'The trains from here to wherever it is we're going.' Unable to cope with this Alice in Wonderland dialogue, I promised that I'd look up the timetable when I went downstairs – and hoped that my voice sounded steady.

I made a sandwich for myself and took it upstairs, so that I could eat it with him. As soon as I came in, he asked impatiently, 'We don't have to dress for this event, do we?' I assured him that we could go exactly as we were. Then, 'What's happening on this thing?'

'What thing?'

'This thing we're travelling on. Where's it going?' He made a sort of circular gesture with his hand. I suggested that perhaps he'd like to sleep now, and he nodded.

I left him then to go and get him a drink, and I picked up the Michael Hollings book which had been lying around in my study. A bookmarker fell out, one of Delia's Christmas cards which I often use as bookmarks – sometimes in the cookery books she has given me, sometimes in her books of spirituality, sometimes elsewhere. This one was very simple; no picture, just an extract from the Quidenham Carmelites' liturgy: 'Creation thrills with joy. Our Lord is coming to clasp the helpless to his heart.' I want to pray, but if I pray it must be for Frank, the helpless one, not for me. He has obviously already embarked on his last journey and doesn't know where it will take him. I remember Dag Hammarskjøld's poem at the beginning of *Markings*:

> I am being driven forward
> Into an unknown land.
> The pass grows steeper,
> The air colder and sharper.
> A wind from my unknown goal
> Stirs the strings
> of expectation.
>
> Still the question:
> Shall I ever get there?
> There where life resounds,
> A clear pure note
> In the silence?[27]

I have always loved *Markings*. (When asked for a list of my favourite books, it comes in my top three; the other two being Eliot's *Four Quartets* and Saint Exupéry's *Le Petit Prince*.) I remember in particular his

> Night is drawing nigh –
> For all that has been – Thanks!
> To all that shall be – Yes!

Hammarskjøld knew how hard that 'Yes' of total acceptance was, yet he insisted:

You dare your yes – and experience a meaning.
You repeat your yes – and all things acquire a meaning.
When everything has a meaning, how can you live
anything but a Yes?

To me that has the ring of truth, but it does not make it any easier.

Monday 27 February 1995

He's gone further away than ever, but still smiles when I come into the room. This morning he announced that he didn't like the driver of the train he was on. Then he began fretting about the weight of the box he had to carry. I told him he mustn't worry, we'd easily find a porter for the box, he only had to bother about himself. Rilke wrote:

My eyes already touch the sunny hill,
going far ahead of the road I have begun.
So we are grasped by what we cannot grasp;
it has its inner light, even from a distance –
and changes us, even if we do not reach it,
into something else, which, hardly sensing it, we
    already are;
a gesture waves us on, answering our own wave –
but what we feel is the wind in our faces.[28]

What would I do without books and poetry, with their accumulated wisdom and insights? They are balm to the weary spirit, shedding light in dark places.

Oddly enough, since they do not seem to have struck people before, everyone is remarking on Frank's radiant smile and beautiful eyes. As he's got weaker and more vulnerable, they've become his channels of communication. In the dim and distant past, he was 'always right', would never accept to be wrong, but now there's a new humility about him which is immensely endearing. 'The only wisdom we can hope to acquire is the wisdom of humility: humility is endless,' wrote Eliot. I cannot remember a time when I have not been consoled by reading Eliot. His poetry has a resonance to which I respond. As I always do in times of particular stress, I am rereading my tattered copy of the *Four Quartets*. 'East Coker' is, for me, the most poignant poem ever written, particularly the last lines in which he speaks of being still, yet at the same time moving:

> Into another intensity
> For a further union, a deeper communion
> Through the dark cold and the empty desolation,
> The wave cry, the wind cry, the vast waters
> Of the petrel and the porpoise. In my end is my
>   beginning.[29]

There's a kind of bubbling noise in his throat – but he seems unaware of it, being still obsessed with those wretched trains. 'Does this train go as far as the terminus?' he has just asked me. 'I expect it does, love.' 'What's it like when you get there?' 'Oh, I'm sure it's very beautiful, there'll be lots of golden light.' 'Will there be yellow daffodils?' he asks, looking at the blooms on the window-sill opposite him. 'I should think there'll be fields and fields of them, and all the other flowers you can think of,' I reply, choking. He looks pleased, then quickly becomes anxious again. 'The train's due at a quarter to four and I think there are just two stops,' he announces busily. 'Don't you think you should go and get your coat? And what about *my* coat? Have *you* got it?' I tell him yes, I have the coat and everything's ready, but he starts worrying about what to do with the glass-fronted wardrobe. He doesn't think he can manage to carry it on his own. 'Leave all that to me,' I say. 'You really don't need to worry about those things, there'll be plenty of people to help.'

Another thought strikes him. 'Will you be coming with me?' he asks. 'As far as I can, yes, love.' 'Well, how far will that be? Will it be all the way?' he presses. 'Let's see how things go, shall we? Why don't you try and sleep now?' But he doesn't want to sleep; he says he must wait for the train to come in, he can't afford to miss it. I don't know why I'm recording all this. A compulsion to try and understand, to find the thread of sanity that still lurks behind his poor addled brain, or perhaps a longing to hold on to what may prove to be the last words he ever speaks to me. I remember the prayer of Philip Toynbee: 'Now may the peace of God fill you with light', and I say it over and over again, till he goes to sleep.

Rang Ruth Ball who had left a message on the answerphone. She was so sympathetic. I'm sure she must be remembering that time a few years ago when her own husband, Freddie, was dying, 'But,' she said, 'though it's terribly cruel, there are moments of pure joy in the midst of it.' There it is again, that mention of joy. So many people have experienced it in these extreme situations. 'Limit situations' they're called – the times when we are driven beyond the limits of our human endurance and yet somehow survive.

Shrove Tuesday, 28 February 1995

The bubbling in his chest continues. It's a bit frightening. But he's fairly lucid again. Joe arrived for an overnight stay and Johnny came again. The latter was overwhelmed by the fact that at this stage when he's in extremis Frank had asked him about his wife, Mary, who is going blind, and had said, 'You will look after her, won't you?' Johnny couldn't get over it. He and Joe both agreed that Frank was being an inspiration to them. Liz, who helps me in the house, also went to say goodbye, and he thanked her for looking after him so well. He is beginning his last farewells now.

Madeleine thinks the bubbling signals the onset of a chest infection. But he's eating well. I had done liver, bacon and onions for Joe – comfort food – and the smell wafted upstairs, making Frank hungry. I mashed a little potato into the gravy for him. He even had a pancake with lemon on it. Quite a meal!

While I was washing up, Angela Matthews rang from Esher – to say that if I need her, she'll drop everything and come. I told her about Frank's hallucination about trains, and she said the same had happened when her father was dying. He had told her, 'I'm not frightened about going off alone on this train, because one day you'll be catching it too and I'll be waiting for you at the other end. Some of us just get an earlier train, that's all.' Angie said that Wendy Craig (no relation) who had lost her husband this time last year had told her that when he died she was filled with great peace and joy, knowing he was with God. I remembered then the interviews I once did for a Radio 4 two-hour marathon on death, way back in the seventies. A woman I visited in Pewsey deplored our Western tendency to dwell on the sorrow and misery of death, and overlook the joy. When her own adored husband died, she said it was as though the whole room was filled with the strains of the last movement of Beethoven's Ninth Symphony, the wonderful 'Ode to Joy'. That feeling had remained with her over the ten years since his death; he had never left her, she assured me. And I thought too about a school-friend who had died of stomach cancer some years ago. Her husband wrote to me that just before she died, she had raised herself in the bed, smiled and said, 'That's the suffering done with. Now for the victory.' Then she lay back and died.

We're not at that stage of understanding yet. Tonight for the first time he didn't know me at all, and it was quite awful.

Ash Wednesday, 1 March 1995

Jeannette, the night nurse, told me he'd been very restless, crying out and shouting in his sleep. This morning he had crunched his tablets with his teeth and taken only a teaspoon of water with them. But he'd gone back to sleep. 'I don't think he'll last much longer,' I ventured. 'No,' she replied, 'the core of life is going from him. There are better places for him to be now.' She thinks he deteriorated still further during last night.

Ash Wednesday, but I shan't be going to church. I have the words running through my head, anyway. I don't need to be reminded of them: 'Remember, man, that thou art dust, and unto dust thou shalt return.' I remember, in 1962 or 1963, when I had gone to Tourcoing to be with André and Françoise after their beautiful little three-year-old Isabelle had been murdered by their live-in help. Ash Wednesday came along, and we all went to the church of St Christophe. But Mme Leman, Françoise's old mother, would not go up with the rest of us to be marked with the ashes. 'There are ashes enough in my heart,' she declared. As there are in mine today.

Frank hasn't opened his eyes, though he did mutter, 'Thank you for everything, Joseph,' when Joe went up to say goodbye. Joe came down and gave me a wordless bear hug – he too was finding the final leave-taking hard. The friendship between us dates back well over thirty years. We had met when I took Mark to the Loreto Convent, Bowdon, for his first day at school; and came upon Joe who was escorting his and Margaret's oldest child, Colette.

Olivia and Julia were the duty nurses. When they saw the state Frank was in today, they decided not to inflict a real wash on him, but just freshen him up. They set about it with great gentleness; they really are very special. Like me, both of them believe that death is not the end but a beginning – and that Frank is already embarked on his voyage of discovery.

Over and over again like a mantra I repeat that little prayer from Philip Toynbee's autobiographical journal, *Part of a Journey*, 'O God of peace, fill him with thy light.'[30] Let him go peacefully now. Philip, who spent a lifetime searching for an elusive God, wrote, among so many other memorable things, 'I have never really reached "Thy Will Be Done". But I know that "Have mercy on us" is not a plea for a mercy which might be with-held, but a reminder of the abundant and ever-present love of God.' How amazingly others continue to help with their deep insights, even when they are themselves long gone. Philip was already an old man when I first met him (in 1977, when I was writing my first book, a biography of Frank Longford), but there was an instant rapport between us. I am grateful for the long, careful review of *Blessings* which he wrote for the *Observer* shortly before he died. He told me (and recorded in *Part of a Journey*) that *Blessings* had arrived at exactly the right moment to help him surmount his own excruciating depressions.

I've just seen the nurses' notes. Their stated aim, 'to keep Mr Craig comfortable and enable him to keep his dignity' is impressive, but oh so chilling.

Three calls have come in from the staff at Nick's day centre in Basingstoke. 'God will carry you if you can't carry yourself,' promised Piedy, the superintendent. I'm always impressed by the deep faith people reveal at such times, the way they somehow find exactly the right consoling thing to say. The sense of human solidarity is awe-inspiring. Shirley has just rung to say that as she left us the other day, she thought, '*There* is one very happy man.' I'm so glad she thought that.

It's 12 noon. Maureen and Peter have arrived and are with him now, but to Maureen's infinite distress he showed no sign of recognition. It must be terrible for her. Yet we know that Frank has already passed beyond pain. The pain is ours now, not his.

Maureen, in tears, says that as they were coming along in the car she kept thinking, 'I was with him when he came into the world [she is one hour older than he], and it looks as though I shall be with him when he leaves it.'

Thursday 2 March 1995

Anne spent ten minutes or so with Frank this morning, and told him that he'd taught her a lot and had made her see things in a different light. She even said he had brought her back to God. I'm sure he heard. The sense of hearing is the last to disappear. I learned that when Betty was dying – I hadn't known but Tom Keeble, our doctor, told me the afternoon before she died. That evening, I held her hand, and told her what Tom had said. 'If you really can still hear, Betty, I want to tell you I love you.' There was the faintest pressure from her hand, and I knew the message had got through.

Jeannette found it difficult to make him take the tablets

last night and impossible this morning. I left a message on Madeleine's answerphone, knowing what the next step is going to be. They have now decided that Frank can no longer take the tablets orally, and have put him on a syringe-driver which delivers a regular measured dose of pain-relieving drugs. Strangely enough, he's been very happy and peaceful today, giving that dazzling smile which has been such a feature of these last weeks. It's quite something. When I went up to see him, he put his hand out to my face, smiled and said once again, 'I love you.'

Friday 3 March 1995

It's snowing and Nick hasn't been able to go to the day centre. Frank had a peaceful night, but yesterday's radiance has disappeared. His face looks sunken; his breathing is uneven. Lilian says his heart-beat is still strong and he could linger on for days. On the other hand, he could go within twenty-four hours. I'm grateful for yesterday, and today at least he is serene. He's obviously not in pain – the syringe-driver has seen to that. He's even been talking to the nurses. Johnny brought Mary to say goodbye, and he greeted her by name, very brightly. She asked him if he had any pain and he shook his head and smiled.

Maureen and Peter are staying over until Anthony can come. (Mark has had to go to Harrogate to give a couple of lectures. He hates being away from us all this week-end.) Madeleine has insisted that I must call her at any hour of the day or night if I need her. She has noticed that his breathing pattern has changed very slightly, but assures me he won't be bothered by it. All we can do now is give him occasional sips of water to keep his mouth moist.

Exactly thirteen years ago I was doing that for Betty. (It

will be the anniversary of her death tomorrow.) I remember half-waking at about 4 a.m. on that last morning, when I was sleeping in her room, and telling myself I ought to get up and get a swab to moisten her tongue. Then I found myself mesmerised by the sound of her breathing – lovely, shallow and innocent, like that of a newborn baby on the threshold of life. I listened entranced. Suddenly the breathing stopped and I sprang completely awake. Leaping out of bed, I realised that she had just died and I couldn't get over how peacefully it had happened. 'I'm glad you saw that death can be beautiful,' said Lilian when she came to certify the death.

The goodbyes are accelerating. Frank's nephews and nieces have made their separate journeys to see him. Our curate, Trevor, and our friend, Desmond, came this morning. Both of them remarked that they had found the experience special and extraordinarily peaceful.

This week's *Tablet* has 'my' Teilhard extract in the Living Spirit column:

> When the signs of age begin to mark my body (and still more when they touch my mind); when the ill that is to diminish me or carry me off strikes from without or is born within me; when the painful moment comes in which I suddenly awaken to the fact that I am ill or growing old; and above all at that last moment when I feel I am losing hold of myself and am absolutely passive within the hands of the great unknown forces that have formed me; in all those dark moments, O God, grant that I may understand that it is you . . . who are painfully parting the fibres of my being in order to penetrate to the very marrow of my substance and bear me away within yourself.

They print also a lovely stanza from George Herbert:

> Whether I fly with angels, fall with dust,
> Thy hands made both, and I am there;
> Thy power and love, my love and trust,
> Make one place ev'rywhere.[31]

Anthony arrived at 6 p.m. At first Frank did not appear to recognise him, which upset me very much. Then light dawned in his eyes, he smiled, and greeted Anthony by name, before lapsing into unconsciousness again. I felt so relieved – it would have been terrible for Anthony not to have had the last precious sign of recognition.

Margaret (Griffiths) rang from St Helens during supper. She and John are going to drive down to see Frank on Sunday. Joe is coming too, and Anthony will be staying over till Monday.

Saturday 4 March 1995

Betty's anniversary, always a sad time. And also, by chance, the fourth anniversary of Frank's lung-cancer operation which had at the time seemed so successful. What price the 'miracle man' now? Maureen and Peter came, Sue and Desmond, and he greeted them all with a smile. As for me, I asked if there was anything he wanted to say to me and he said, 'Yes' quite emphatically.

'What is it then?'

'I – love – you,' he said slowly and carefully, enunciating the words as if he was trying to be sure he had got them right. In the event, they *were* the last words he would ever speak, and perhaps he had come back from a long way away, in order to say them. I told him how much all of us loved him and he smiled. I also said that if he was going on that journey first, he must make sure he was there to meet me when it was my turn. He nodded quite vigorously before going back to sleep.

Anthony and I worked hard to clear all his papers and arrange them in the new filing cabinet which Peter has sensibly persuaded me to buy. One thing we unearthed was the memorial card I'd had printed after Mother's death in 1972: *'Life is only for Love. Time is only that we may find God.'* It's a quotation from St Bernard of Clairvaux, and I may well use it again for Frank's card.

Mary O'Hara's anthology[32] is on the desk in front of me, open at an extract from Lewis's *A Grief Observed*. Lewis suggests that the dead also feel the pains of separation and that this may be what is meant by purgatory. Whatever the truth of it, to us it seems that death comes: 'As love cut short; like a dance stopped in mid-career or a flower with its head unluckily snapped off.' Bereavement, on the other hand, is 'a universal and integral part of our experience of love. It follows marriage as normally as marriage follows courtship or as autumn follows summer. It is not a truncation of the process but one of its phases; not the interruption of the dance, but the next figure.' Above all, we must resist the temptation to 'fall back to loving our past, or our memory, or our sorrow, or our relief from sorrow, or our own love'. In this, the final figure of the dance, we must learn to love the spiritual essence, the real self of the one we have loved.

Frank was very restless. I pressed the booster button on the syringe-driver but it did not seem to calm him.

Sunday 5 March 1995

He remained restless all last evening and throughout the night. The night nurse rang Colin, who prescribed a sedative. This morning he came round and increased the amount of morphine for the syringe-driver. I'm relieved – they've been fairly successful in containing the pain so far, and I'd hate to think of it getting the upper hand now. I could not help thinking this morning, when I saw him sprawled unconscious on the bed, how much he is now in the hands of strangers, passive, being 'led where he would not go'. All part of that letting-go process which surely for him is nearing its end. There is not much else he can let go of. Except the last threads of his life.

Margaret and John came. I was touched that they should drive hundreds of miles just to be with us for a couple of hours. Frank actually recognised them and smiled, though he could no longer talk. Poor Margaret was very upset when she came downstairs. She said, 'I came to say goodbye to him, but I couldn't get any words out. I was too choked.' She has known Frank for nearly fifty years. I remember introducing them in 1947 when she came to stay with me when I was a student in Oxford. I had to go to some meeting or other, and he took Margaret to see Shaw's *Heartbreak House*, and to dinner – at the British Restaurant! It was all he could afford in those days, and in any case there wasn't much choice in the early post-war years. (Frank and I had once spent an evening going all over Oxford in search of egg and chips! We found it in the end too.)

Sue sat with him for a while in the afternoon and brought a few catkins to enliven the daffodils on the window-sill. As he still seemed restless, I rang Colin – who came instantly. He seems to think that the amount of sedation was actually about right, but once again has insisted that I must ring him if there is any change. How shall I ever be able to repay so much kindness and support? Everybody at the surgery has been so very kind – far beyond the call of duty.

Frank was fairly blank tonight, seeming to recognise us

for a few seconds, no more. But he held my hand tight – his grip was still firm. Nick joined Anthony and me in the bedroom, but became very distressed when Frank looked at him without recognition. 'What is it?' he wailed. 'What's happening to him?' Tears streamed down his cheeks. Then with an angry 'You look after him', he dashed out of the room. Anthony followed him and asked him if he understood what was going to happen. Yes, he said, Dad was going to die, just like Auntie Betty, and wouldn't be coming back – ever. Anthony said, 'But you'll still be here, in your new house and your nice new room, and Mum will be here for you to take care of just as Dad always did.' Poor Nick, he and his father were so close. Frank was always thinking of ways to please him, things to buy for him, games that he might be able to play. He'd even taught him some simple conjuring tricks of which Nick was immensely proud.

As I sat by Frank tonight, my mind went back to our first meeting. It was my first term up at Oxford at the end of 1946 – the time that is always known as Oxford's golden age, when the university was full of exciting new talent, and the ex-servicemen and women were returning from the war. My friend Hazel and I – mere, callow ex-schoolgirls – had gone down to the Catholic chaplaincy social club in search of 'interesting men'. As we arrived, a boy with unbelievably wavy, dark hair came down the stairs carrying a kettle. 'Any men left up there?' I asked brassily, and he looked at me in disgust. But later, at the Sunday evening social, he asked me to dance – several times – and he was one of the best dancers I'd ever come across. When I came back to Oxford after the Christmas vacation, someone said, 'Do you remember that good-looking dark boy you danced with at the Chaplaincy Social? He dropped dead during the vac.' I was devastated. But on the following Sunday, at the chaplaincy social, to my consternation, there was Frank

– again asking me to dance. I stared at him, open-mouthed. 'But you're supposed to be dead,' I spluttered inanely. I was so relieved to see him. (I heard afterwards that it was another of my dancing partners who had died.) Before long we had started going out together. I was eighteen, he nineteen.

All that was almost half a century ago, and now he really is going to die. But I'm grateful for the long reprieve. There were many times when we all but came unstuck, and nobody could ever have called us soul mates. But affection and trust kept us together even when the relationship was under strain, and neither of us ever seriously contemplated giving up on the other. In any case there was Nick to think of. We wouldn't knowingly have done anything to hurt him.

Jeannette is on night-duty tonight. She feels that the end is very near, and is confident it will be peaceful.

Monday 6 March 1995

9 p.m. – I've come downstairs for a few moments relief, while Anthony keeps vigil by Frank's bedside. It's been a harrowing day, and it seems very unlikely that Frank will see it out. I can't just sit still drumming my fingers, I must concentrate on writing this. Somehow I must account for every part of this final day.

I woke at 4.30 a.m. to the sound of noisy and laboured breathing. Anthony was already up and in the room with Frank. Jeannette administered a booster dose and rang the surgery to ask Jenny if she'd come in earlier than usual to fill the syringe which was getting rather low. I went back to bed till just before 7 a.m. when Jeannette left and I resumed my own vigil.

Anthony decided to stay until Joe came, so as not to leave

me alone. When Colin arrived, he warned me that it was now only a matter of hours. Bronchial pneumonia has set in. Colin changed the drugs and gave him more morphine. The breathing sounds awful, but Madeleine says he will not be suffering. If one ignores the noise, he actually looks quite peaceful.

Joe came and Anthony left for Gloucester – he moved there recently from Bristol, to be nearer to his work – to pick up some things for a more prolonged stay. He is going to take a week's leave. While Joe sat with Frank and the nurses did whatever remained to be done, I blindly chopped vegetables for soup and made a chicken pasta salad and a casserole, to ensure that there'd be enough food for whoever turned up today. After all there would be at least seven of us – Maureen and Peter, Joe, Anthony, Mark, Nick, myself. Though I don't suppose any of us will have any appetite.

Anne came on the way back from a particularly harrowing visit to her mother. I put on the 'Laudate' cassette of Taizé chants while waiting for Madeleine and Jenny to come downstairs. It seemed fitting somehow. Anne thought the music extraordinarily beautiful and when Madeleine and Jenny came and heard the 'Veni Sancte Spiritus', they just stood and listened, stunned by it. Both of them asked if I could get them a cassette to use in their work with people who are dying.

Anne went upstairs for a final goodbye – and to tell Frank that she is going to plant primroses in the Marsh Benham churchyard in his memory. She left a little silver Celtic cross on the bedspread. When he had gone, I went up to the bedroom, and didn't leave him all day until a few minutes ago. I'm so tired I scarcely know what I am doing.

He's been on a bigger dose of morphine today. His breathing has sounded awful but Madeleine insists that he is beyond being aware of it. I spent the afternoon and early evening singing Taizé chants to him, very low, 'Ubi Caritas', 'Confitemini Domino', 'Lord, Hear My Prayer'. There was an undeniable solace in repeating these, like a sad valediction. I'm getting strength from somewhere, though I ache with weariness.

Mark came for several hours, and Maureen and Peter were with him this evening, silently praying the rosary. At five minutes to eight, Anthony brought up a card that had been pushed through the letter-box. It was from the Julian group which I intermittently attend and they had delivered it minutes before their fortnightly meditation meeting. 'With very much love from us all,' it said. 'You will be much in our prayers this evening and throughout the night.' There are prayers on the card: 'The steadfast love of the Lord never ceases; His mercies never come to an end; they are new every morning; great is thy faithfulness.' And that magnificent passage from Isaiah which I love:

> Fear not, for I have redeemed you; I have called you by your name; you are mine. When you pass through the waters, I will be with you; and when you pass through the rivers, they will not sweep over you. When you walk through the fire, you will not be burned; the flames will not set you ablaze. For I am the Lord your God, the Holy One of Israel, your Saviour. (Isa. 43:2–3)

Were there ever more comforting words than those?

Anthony took Nick over to Ellen's house, having suggested that staying at home this evening would be too harrowing for him. Ellen has handled him wonderfully throughout the crisis, talking him through Frank's coming death. He has told her he understands what is happening and knows that Dad is going to go to heaven.

'To be with Dave,' prompted Ellen, referring to her

husband who had been killed in a terrible glider crash a few years previously.

'And Auntie Betty,' added Nick, of his own accord.

'And he'll be able to look after you from where he's going.'

'I know,' said Nick.

'And you'll be the man of the house and look after Mum and make Dad proud of you.'

'I know,' nodded Nick.

Midnight

It's finished. *Consummatum est.* I write this, sitting by Frank's body which is slowly growing cold. I shall spend the night here; I can't leave him now.

I came upstairs after the half-hour I spent writing this at 9 p.m. Anthony was with him. As I sat down again by the bed, Frank's breathing suddenly became less troubled. I stroked his hand and sang 'Ubi Caritas et Amor' over and over again to him, 'Where there is love and loving kindness, there God is.' Singing brought a kind of relief from sorrow. I had rung Ellen and asked if she and Tracey would bring Nick back at about 9.45 p.m., and Anthony now sat, lying across the top of the stairs, waiting for them. I could see his hand from where I sat. Just before they were due to arrive, he joined me in here, and we saw that the white discharge was no longer coming out of Frank's nose and that he sounded merely as though he was snoring. I said, 'When Nick comes, I think you could bring him in to say goodbye. Dad looks quite peaceful, it won't be too distressing for him.' Anthony, however, thought that Nick should have his bath first, while Ellen and Tracey came in to say goodbye to Frank.

I heard Nick lumber upstairs. Frank's breathing was

gentle now, and I knew with absolute certainty that the end was at hand. As Ellen and Tracey came up, the breathing faded to the gentle, peaceful rhythm that had preceded Betty's death. I was still singing 'Ubi Caritas'. He seemed to give a slight smile, the merest hint of a gurgle, a stream of white fluid gushed out of his nostrils, and the breathing stopped. He was dead. Or rather, was he already, in Hopkins' words, 'immortal diamond'?

> In a flash, at a trumpet crash,
> I am all at once what Christ is, since he was what I
>   am, and
> This Jack, joke, poor potsherd, patch, matchwood,
>   immortal diamond
>   Is immortal diamond.[33]

Ellen tapped gently on the door. 'He's just this second gone,' I whispered. Tracey and Anthony came in too and we all silently embraced. No words were possible. Jan, the nurse, arrived at that crucial moment. It was 9.55 p.m.

Frank looked unbelievably peaceful, as though he had just fallen asleep, as indeed he had. 'When the knot of the heart is cut, mortal becomes immortal' – the line comes unbidden from I know not where. He is at peace now.

> Fear no more the heat of the sun
> Nor the furious winter's rages;
> Thou thy worldly task hast done,
> Home art gone and ta'en thy wages.[34]

Nick came out of the bathroom and Anthony put a protective arm round him as he brought him in to the bedroom. He kissed Frank nervously and held his hand, stroking it with his other one. It was a poignant moment, with all of us there to support him. Then he went downstairs with Ellen and Tracey, understanding at last broke through, and he wept.

Jan had summoned the duty doctor. While we waited, she told me that Frank had been happy throughout the previous night. He had kept 'smiling such a beautiful smile', she said, that she was sure he knew that he was surrounded by love.

The duty doctor – Nick Yates – confirmed the death and remarked on how peaceful Frank looked. When I told him I'd been singing to him all afternoon and evening, he said that Frank would certainly have been aware of it – with that sense of hearing that remains almost to the end. I was glad then that I'd told him I loved him at frequent intervals throughout the day, though there had been no recognition or acknowledgment on his part.

Downstairs with Ellen and Tracey, Nick was breaking his heart. Nick Yates hugged him and told him it was a good thing to cry and he shouldn't be afraid to do so. Then Nick, one of nature's innocents, forgot his misery when Ellen and Tracey said they'd take him out for the day tomorrow! Anthony rang to break the news to Maureen, Peter and Mark – and arranged with the funeral directors to come tomorrow at 10 a.m. Ellen and Tracey will come and collect Nick at 9.30 a.m.

So, now I'm alone with Frank's body in the calm of the night. It's still hard to grasp that he's gone. Somehow I keep expecting him to move or open his eyes. I haven't yet fully taken in the fact that it's over, that his strength and support will no longer be there for me. But I'm glad for him, that he is at rest. I sense the presence of God, the oneness of all things, and a profound peace all around – and I am not unhappy. Tomorrow will be worse. Tomorrow I have to face reality.

In fact, I kept watch with Frank through the night. I couldn't bring myself to leave him. He looked so peaceful – one could imagine that he was still breathing and would soon wake up. The night was icy and though I wrapped myself up in a coat I was still cold.

Where is he now, I wonder? Somewhere in 'the dark backward and abysm of Time'? There are some beautiful words in the *Upanishads* which express all one's hopes for one's dead loved ones:

> There is a bridge between Time and Eternity; and this bridge is Atman, the Spirit of Man. Neither day nor night cross that bridge, nor old age, nor death, nor sorrow. Evil and sin cannot cross that bridge, the world of the Spirit is pure. This is why, when the bridge has been crossed, the eyes of the blind can see, the wounds of the wounded are healed, and the sick man becomes whole from his sickness. To one who goes over that bridge the night becomes like unto day, because in the world of the Spirit there is a light which is everlasting.[35]

I hope Frank now knows something of that everlasting light. I pray my favourite prayer from the *Upanishads* for him:

> Lead me from the Unreal to the Real,
> Lead me from Darkness to Light,
> Lead me from Death to Immortality.

Came down at 7 a.m. when I heard Anthony moving around. Maureen and Peter came about 8 a.m. (they were staying nearby with friends), but couldn't bring themselves to go upstairs and see the body. They had already said goodbye to him yesterday. Madeleine came too. She had been at the Julian group's meditation session and had told them about the sense of utter peace in the house, and about the Taizé chants.

Tracey came for Nick. The very worst moment of all was when Anthony and I went downstairs and the undertakers arrived to take Frank away. I put the Taizé cassette on, turned my back to the door – and howled like a baby. Anthony too was crying. What was it Hopkins wrote,

No worst, there is none. Pitched past pitch of grief,
More pangs will, schooled at forepangs, wilder wrung.
Comforter, where is your comforting?

It was terrible. There we both were, frantic, searching for a consolation which was nowhere to be found.

Anthony was marvellous. He had to deal with all the telephoning, and later, with all the incoming calls. I couldn't cope. The funeral is to be on Monday at St Francis de Sales church. I dread it.

Friends kept on ringing, and the house was full all day. Tracey drove Nick back from his day out. He was very cheerful; she'd let him buy some lottery tickets for himself and a card for me. He'd chosen the card himself and told Ellen what he wanted to write on it. (He knows his alphabet but cannot put the letters into words by himself. He needs someone to spell the message out, letter by letter.) 'Dear Mum,' he wrote in his big, sprawling capitals. 'I will love you always and I want to help. Love Nick xxxx'

Wednesday 8 March 1995

Anthony went to register the death. Mark arrived at about

119

1 p.m. and took over the task of telephoning and fielding calls, and of writing some essential letters. He said that last night Timmy had 'talked to God and Grandpa' and said, 'We still love you, Grandpa.'

We went down to the churchyard to see the spot that has been allocated to us – a lovely, peaceful place. Then we went to order a large spray of spring flowers. When Nick arrived home from the day centre, Anthony and I drove him straight over to Ellen's to have supper again, and I took with me the liturgy which I've prepared for next Monday. Ellen is going to make a booklet of it and I'll get the copies printed on Friday.

Various friends and people from the parish have offered to put up relatives and friends who are coming for the funeral. I told John Nelson, our parish priest, that I'd like to ask my Anglican friend, David Winter, to give the address; and he has agreed, was delighted in fact. John, Fr Seamus, and Peter Bowe from Douai Abbey are going to concelebrate the requiem mass.

The evening was spent, one way and another, on the telephone. Mark – who had not been there at the actual time of Frank's death – took the decision to go and view his Dad's body in the chapel of rest. He found it intolerably distressing and broke down completely. I'm glad I didn't go.

Letters, cards and flowers have started arriving.

Friday 10 March 1995

Very busy. Lots of letters. We collected the liturgy draft from Ellen when we took Nick to spend the evening with her yesterday. She had made a splendid job of the booklet. Today, David came over to talk about the homily he will be giving at the funeral mass. Trevor says that Carol from the Julian group (a former BBC singer) will sing the 'Pie Jesu' and the 'In Paradisum' at the end. I hesitate between the Fauré 'Pie Jesu', and the Lloyd Webber. I know the Fauré is beautiful, but I do love the Lloyd Webber one. I think Frank would have preferred that one to be sung at his funeral.

Saturday 11 March 1995

This limbo period between death and burial is hard to bear. Suddenly I am bereft of signposts.

The letters and cards continue to flood in. So many people manage to find just the right words of consolation. One long letter, from my lifelong friend, Mary Tuck, recalls our Oxford undergraduate days and 'the handsome, curly-headed boy who loved you so'. I was glad of her letter, for our friendship goes back to our very earliest days in kindergarten and has grown with the passing years. Over sixty years, in fact. 'There are no words really, are there?' she wrote. 'But I guess we've known each other longer than anyone else, so we don't need words. Love to my sister-friend. I know you must be suffering but I know too you will manage with the grace, courage, intelligence and loving heart you have always shown.' An unlooked-for tribute, which I shall always cherish.[36] There was a moving one too from Anthony's friend, Anne, enclosing two poems of Christina Rossetti. The first, the well-known sonnet:

> Remember me when I am gone away,
>   Gone far away into the silent land;
>   When you can no more hold me by the hand,
> Nor I half turn to go, yet turning stay.
> Remember me when no more day by day

You tell me of our future that you planned:
 Only remember me; you understand
It will be late to counsel then or pray.
Yet, if you should forget me for a while
 And afterwards remember, do not grieve:
 For if the darkness and corruption leave
A vestige of the thoughts that once I had,
Better by far you should forget and smile
 Than that you should remember and be sad.

The second poem Anne sent was the song:

When I am dead, my dearest,
 Sing no sad songs for me
Plant thou no roses at my head,
 Nor shady cypress tree:
Be the green grass above me
 With showers and dewdrops wet;
And, if thou wilt, remember,
 And, if thou wilt, forget.
I shall not see the shadows,
 I shall not feel the rain;
I shall not hear the nightingale
 Sing on, as if in pain;

And dreaming through the twilight
 That doth not rise nor set,
Haply I may remember
 And haply may forget.

Last night, I found a packet of old letters in Frank's pyjama drawer. He'd kept my letters, right from our first meeting; even the first rather formal ones when we were still unsure of our feelings. Then gradually the feelings ripened into love. One line from a letter I sent from Dumfries after we were engaged is particularly poignant now, 'I so long to be with you till death us do part.' How easily and unthinkingly that phrase tripped off my pen in 1950, having no relevance to reality. Dying was something we hadn't begun to imagine.

We have all written cards to accompany the floral tribute and I took them round to the florist. Anthony's and Mark's expressed their deep grief and paid moving tribute to Frank's steadfastness and love for them. I asked Nick to tell me what he would like to say. He dictated, 'I love you and miss you, Dad.' He wrote the letters as I spelled them out. When he had finished, 'That's it, then,' he said, putting down the pen with an air of finality. 'That's Dad finished.' It sounds hurtful but it wasn't; it was just Nick sorting things out for himself in his own inimitable way. He likes things to be cut and dried. He was a bit like that when Betty died. It's difficult if not downright impossible to explain to him what is going to happen at the funeral on Monday. How can one put it in terms he will understand? On one level, he doesn't seem to understand any of it. But perhaps one should be grateful for the fact.

Flowers arrived from France, and from our (how am I ever going to get used to saying 'my', not 'our'?) new next-door neighbours. Joy, my hairdresser, gave me a lovely climbing rose called 'New Dawn'. I don't think we ever had climbing roses before.

Sunday 12 March 1995

The dreaded day comes nearer. I keep telling myself that the 'thing' that will be brought into the church tomorrow is only a shell; not Frank at all. Anthony, to console me – and

Nick – says tomorrow is a time when people will all be saying loving things about Dad, and when he will be laid to rest in a beautiful place where we can all go and visit him and talk to him and remember. I'm going to miss having Anthony here. He's been a great comfort.

Nick went to Ellen's for lunch. John Nelson came in the afternoon and brought a letter from (Bishop) Crispian, (an old friend from BBC days), explaining that he's going to Rome tomorrow, so can't be with us but will be thinking of us. I drove to Thatcham to collect Nick and found Maureen and Peter already in the house when I got back. My cousins, Mollie and Bill, came soon after and Desmond brought Frances Donnelly round – it seemed so strange that she was staying with them rather than with me, as she usually does. Nick joined us. I think he feels more need of company at present.

Monday 13 March 1995

D-day. Slept badly and had a nightmare. In the morning I made one last effort to get through to Tendzin Choegyal in Dharamsala (the lines to India have been impossible over the last few days, so I hadn't yet told him of Frank's death). This time I reached him within seconds. He was full of sympathy. I told him I knew all the philosophical arguments against clinging to the past, but they didn't stop me crying all the time, and he said, 'Of course you must cry. Let the tears come, but don't let your heart be heavy. Frank is at peace.' It was good to talk to Tendzin on this traumatic day: I value his friendship greatly.

Mark and the family arrived; Timmy wearing a waistcoat and a black tie and looking very chic. He's been 'talking to Grandpa' again, telling him not to worry, he still loves him.

He told Mark he'd dreamed of picking up a toy telephone and hearing Grandpa's voice talking French!

It was a rare, smiling March day and the funeral went off very well. It was at one and the same time harrowing and incredibly beautiful. The church was packed; virtually standing room only. Worst moment of all was seeing the coffin arrive, then having to walk behind it into the church. I wanted to run away.

I had chosen the liturgy myself. Donald Coggan did the first reading from the Book of Wisdom. Then, after 'The Lord is My Shepherd', Joe read from St Paul to the Romans. Peter (Bowe) read the beautiful verses from St John's Gospel, 'I am the Way, the Truth and the Life'. David's homily was as good as I had known it would be. I'll try and reproduce it, though the recording which I have of the whole service was not very successful.

In the Old Testament reading this morning, we heard the phrase 'the righteous shall shine like the sun'. I did not know when I chose the phrase for my homily that the sun would be shining, but there is something so right and appropriate that we should be gifted with such a rare, sunny day in March. 'The righteous shall shine like the sun.' The word that seems to fit Frank better than any is that word 'righteous', though some of you may cringe and I know he would have rejected it out of hand. We instantly think of false piety, being holier-than-thou, do-goodery, and that awful phrase, '*self*-righteous'. But for a few minutes I'd like to snatch that lovely word, 'righteous', away from its denigrators and apply it to the man whom we remember with thanksgiving before God today. To say Frank was a righteous man does not mean that Frank was always right. Nor does it suggest he was particularly holy or deeply spiritual or devout. A righteous person doesn't necessarily enjoy church ritual or worship. No, righteousness has to do with our choices in life. Righteousness is about doing right, doing what God requires of us. And in that sense the word kept coming into my mind as Mary and I talked about Frank and as she showed me the letters and cards which were coming in from friends and colleagues after his death last week. He was, it seemed to me, a man who wanted, in every situation he encountered, to do what was right. He was indeed never particularly devout, he didn't theorise or speculate, still less agonise over theology or ethics. He simply sought to do what was right, and to do it one day at a time.

At work, Frank was a very distinguished chemist and metallurgist. He had no driving ambition, but his career simply went up and up and up. One of his former staff wrote how much he had been guided by Frank's wise advice throughout his own career; another wrote that he was 'fair, just, always a person you could trust'. He was 'quiet, firm, single-minded but never ruthless', wrote a third. A man, in fact, who went out of his way to help in practical ways – which he would have said were obvious. And all of that is what the gospel means by 'a righteous person'.

Or, take the family. When Paul was born, he never flinched. Whatever he may have felt, he simply did what was necessary, what was right. He wouldn't have thought that remarkable or admirable or worthy of canonisation. Someone in the family said he was always rock-like in a crisis. A righteous man.

His was a case in which you really could speak of 'simple faith'. Frank was uncomplicated; his faith was to be applied rather than to be agonised over.

And then, finally, the man who had been such a rock-like support to others – the last years of his life were devoted to working for Mencap, because he felt he had been given so much he needed to repay the debt to society – lost the ability to support even himself. That may well have been his ultimate test in the matter of doing what was right. And in that situation, he never protested, never complained, never said 'Why me?' He just did what was right – which included putting a Valentine in *The Times* just a week or so before he died – and following it up with a present for Mary from the Argos catalogue. That was the only option left to him, and that at least he could do without stirring from his bed.

Frank simply made light of what he was enduring – the proper, theological word for it is 'resignation', not in the sense of giving up, but of trusting acceptance. And he remained cheerful through it all.

So we have this shy, generous, unassuming man; who felt socially, perhaps, sometimes overshadowed, sometimes excluded, but who showed in those last eight months of his life, the true heart of his character. Not by what he said, but by what he was.

As one of their friends said on the last day of his life, 'I owe a lot to Frank. He has brought me back to God.'

So, a righteous man. A man who simply and uncomplicatedly, throughout his life, sought to do what was right. And today we remember him at the place, and within the sacrament, where he would wish to be remembered, and where we remember the Righteous One whose body was broken and blood shed for us, 'by whose wounds we are healed'. The One who said – and made the promise possible – 'Then the righteous will shine like the sun in the kingdom of my Father.'

Shine, Frank, *shine!*

Fr John said afterwards, 'Your choice of speaker was inspired.' He himself handled everything with great dignity and openness – we were all impressed.

I had written the bidding prayers, and chosen friends to read them who were close to Frank and myself at the end: Trevor, Anne, Sue, Gerard, Ellen, Mary O'Hara and Madeleine. (Maureen and Peter felt it would be too much of an ordeal for them.) Then we sang the lovely prayer of St Francis, 'Make Me a Channel of Your Peace', which has always been a special favourite. This is the sung version:

> Make me a channel of your peace,
> Where there is hatred, let me bring your love.
> Where there is injury, your pardon, Lord.
> And where there's doubt, true faith in you.
>
> Make me a channel of your peace.
> Where there's despair in life
> let me bring hope.
> Where there is darkness, only light
> And where there's sadness, ever joy.
>
> O Master, grant that I may never seek
> so much to be consoled as to console;
> to be understood as to understand
> to be loved as to love with all my soul.
>
> Make me a channel of your peace.
> It is in pardoning that we are pardoned,
> in giving to all men that we receive,
> and in dying that we're born to eternal life.

Almost everyone in the church went up to receive Communion, whether Catholic, Anglican, Baptist, Methodist or agnostic. I could see so many old friends who had come from far away. The father-figure in my life, Frank Longford, was there, almost ninety and nearly blind. He had travelled all the way from Sussex across London. Fortunately he met my cousin, Anne Forbes, on the train from London, and she was able to give him a hand. Four old school-friends came from St Helens; other friends from Altrincham days were there. Many came from London; including Giles, my editor from HarperCollins. There were Fi and Gwen, two friends we'd made on that last Caribbean cruise, when – had we but known it – the count-down had already begun; old friends like Francis and Angela Matthews who'd driven over from Esher, and Pek Leng who'd come from Barnet with a huge bouquet of arum lilies; lots of Mencap people; the plumber, the carpenter and the ex-builder who've been helping us in the new house; nearly all the nurses who had looked after Frank; Lilian and at least three of the pharmacists from the surgery. During the lengthy Communion, 'Ubi Caritas' was sung, and that of course was one time when I completely lost my composure and wept. Memories of that last day of Frank's life came crowding in. After the Communion, Carol Foster-Fletcher sang Lloyd Webber's 'Pie Jesu'. What a glorious voice. Perfect. I felt overwhelmed with gratitude.

Then the awesome Final Commendation, as the coffin was slowly taken out of the church. Even at the best of times, when I'm not personally involved, the onset of this prayer makes me weepy, and I was absolutely dreading it. I have often thought that the veils some widows wear at funerals were intended for this very moment when they cannot prevent the raw grief from showing. I *knew*, of course I knew – or so I kept assuring myself – it wasn't Frank, imprisoned in that stark wooden coffin. The knowledge helped me through.

Many people followed us to the churchyard. The sun shone and the ceremony was full of grace and peace. Again, somehow I didn't experience it as painful and was able to sprinkle the coffin with holy water as it lay in the open grave – 'Goodbye, my love, be with God.' It was an idyllic spot in which to be buried, and one day I hope to join him there. Meanwhile, as Anthony keeps telling Nick, 'We shall go there often and talk to Dad.'

One thing everyone seemed agreed on was that it had been a beautiful service, many going so far as to say it was the most inspiring and unforgettable they had ever attended. Gerry Gibbons, Frank's friend from their old youth club days in Farnborough, said it had turned him upside down. He had always argued that ceremonial was unnecessary, but today was forced to acknowledge that he'd been wrong. For me, ceremonial on such a solemn occasion is terribly important. It marks a rite of passage.

At the reception later, people seemed to enjoy themselves, as people usually do at funerals. Timmy was very grown-up in his new waistcoat, and two-year-old Dani (well, she's almost two) distinguished herself by taking off all her clothes and running around the parish hall completely starkers. There was a huge amount of food – the parish ladies had put on a tremendous spread. 'You are part of our community and we're glad to do it,' they assured me. (Which was very charitable of them, as I'm ashamed to admit I do nothing at all for the parish. I'm the original non-joiner, as they must know by now.) I owe so much to so many and don't know how I can begin to thank them.

Returned home with the children and grandchildren – and when Mark and his family had gone home, and Anthony had gone to bed, I put on an Inti Illimani cassette and began to write this account. The plaintive, panpipe music suited my mood. Then Maureen and Peter arrived –

to stay – and we sat and mulled over the day's events. Now they too have gone to bed and I'm finishing this to the strains of the Allegri 'Miserere' and the Verdi 'Requiem'. Sublime music.

Tuesday 14 March 1995

Maureen, Peter and I went down to the churchyard. Another lovely sunny day, though, unlike yesterday, windy and cold. Had a better chance to look at the spray of flowers lying on the grave – red roses, carnations, tulips, daffodils and tiger lilies. They made a glorious palette of colour, and the four cards spoke volumes. There was Maureen's wreath also which I hadn't really seen yesterday – she'd made it herself with spring flowers and last year's leaves from the garden at our old house. To my surprise there were also a few other sheaves from neighbours old and new. It was quiet and tranquil in the churchyard, under the giant cedars and cypresses, but I was suddenly overwhelmed with grief and couldn't stay.

Wednesday 15 March 1995

Went again to the churchyard, then round to Trevor's with various letters of thanks. He said that Carol, who had sung the 'Pie Jesu' so magnificently, had told him she'd sung it all to Nick, who was gazing at her in wonder throughout. At the end he broke into a smile and clapped! Trust Nick! But I think a lot of people felt like applauding.

Carol wrote to me herself and said,

Although some of us never met Frank, at the Julian group

we grew to care very much for him, and held you both in our thoughts and prayers. It seems strange that the death and funeral of a man I didn't know should have such a profound effect on me, but that is how it is. I feel it a great privilege to have been part of such a wonderful celebration of Frank's life and death. The church seemed full of love and warmth and hope and even joy.

Trevor says he now believes the Julian group came into existence for the sake of Frank – it seems to have found its cohesion and purpose through him.

Friday 17 March 1995

Today at last I was 'signed-off' by the eye surgeon. He says my left eye is now completely clear and my sight is above the legal requirement for driving. But the right eye is deteriorating and he thinks it too will need to be 'done' before long. Maybe in a year.

Maureen and Peter left today, and it seemed strange being in an empty house. (Nick is at his day centre.) They have been very supportive, but I must stand on my own feet from now on, and start living normally.

Not that I was on my own for long. Various friends arrived with bouquets of flowers, and Trevor brought me a folding prayer-stool – a delayed Christmas present. The rector of Highclere brought me a sheet of prayers. Shirley rang and invited me to lunch, as did Sarah Kennedy. Impossible – as yet – to be lonely with so many friends about. My main feeling right now is one of total exhaustion. Shirley advises being kind to myself and not driving myself to do anything I don't want to. Frances, from whom I had a letter this morning, agrees. She has been a Cruse counsellor for some time and says, 'Mourning can be a very draining experience. What all bereaved people say to me is how exhausted they feel. So I hope you are being extremely kind to yourself.' She adds:

> I think about Frank constantly and have a real sense of him being at peace. The Sunday before he died, India [her eight-year-old daughter] and I went to the family service at the Methodist chapel, and, as usual, we were asked at the start of the service who we wanted to dedicate it to. Quite unprompted, India put up her hand and said she wanted to pray for 'Mary Craig's husband, Frank, who is dying of cancer!' So you can see we were with Frank in our thoughts right to the end.

Margaret rang from St Helens. She said that during the requiem on Monday it had been 'glorious spring' both outside and inside the church – as the sun streamed in she had been overwhelmed by a sense of joy. So very many people seem to have felt that joy and been surprised by it. How amazed Frank would have been to know that his death had affected so many so strongly.

Anthony and I listened to the recording of the funeral service, but though the music has recorded well, the spoken part, including David's homily, is much less clear. Anthony went to bed after we'd listened, and I got out Trevor's prayer-stool and listened to one complete side of the Taizé cassette. I somehow wanted to stay there all night in that calm stillness and peace. I know that, though inevitably I shall soon return to what passes for normality, with no time to call my own, I must never forget that this time has had its own undeniable richness. These days so full of anguish are nevertheless precious for the kernel of joy they contain. I have a distinct awareness of the world being underpinned and held in place by love. Like the fourteenth-century Julian of Norwich's vision of the whole world being a hazelnut in the hand of God:

> He showed me a little thing, the size of a hazelnut, in the palm of my hand, and it was as round as a ball. I looked at it with my mind's eye and I thought, 'What can this be?' And answer came, 'It is all that is made.' I marvelled that it could last, for I thought it might have crumbled to nothing, it was so small. And the answer came into my mind, 'It lasts and ever shall because God loves it.' And all things have being through the love of God.[37]

Sunday 19 March 1995

That kind of awareness – however appealing – does not soften (nor, I suppose, should it) the ever-present sense of loss. Certain things predominate: the new sense of insecurity, loss of safe landmarks, unpredictability. And the sudden, recurring pangs of separation and loss. It takes little to trigger a spasm of desolation: the sight of the plastic tumbler by the bathroom washbowl, a specially small one that was light enough for him to hold; his now unwanted hearing-aid; an old photograph of the way he was when I first met him; the sound of Alistair Cooke's 'Letter from America' on Radio 4 to which he had always listened on a Sunday morning. I suppose that in time these gusts of pain will diminish in force. Meanwhile, they will come and must be endured – in the full certainty that they will pass. The Buddhists say of distractions in meditation: 'Watch them happen, watch their passage across the screen of your mind, and watch them disappear.' The same applies here. In any case I wouldn't want to run away from grief – it is the price we have to pay for loving. Like Milton grieving for Lycidas:

> But, oh, the heavy change, now thou art gone,
> Now thou art gone, and never must return.

Mass at St Francis' yesterday was in memory of Frank. Afterwards, a lot of people expressed their condolences. Many had been at the requiem and had found it an unforgettable experience. One lady asked if Frank's death hadn't been a merciful release, and I said, no, it hadn't been like that. Yet, when I think about it, for Frank at least it probably was. As Anthony said, 'I think Dad had had enough.' Strange to think that this time last year he was all right, apart from tiredness and backache.

Margaret Cheetham drove over from Cheltenham to spend the day with me – Joe was unfortunately unable to come with her. She thought the house seemed very peaceful. When she left, at six-ish, Nick and I were on our own for the first time since Frank's death. This evening I read Alan Bennett's delightful diaries, *Writing Home*. He writes:

> The majority of people perform well in a crisis and when the spotlight is on them; it's on the Sunday afternoons of this life, when nobody is looking, that the spirit falters.[38]

How well Bennett understands the human condition. I suspect that a lot of Sunday afternoons lie ahead.

Wednesday 22 March 1995

I've now survived three nights. The days seem a bit long, though, and I seem to be paralysed by an inability to choose between various activities. I suppose I must give it time and not expect too much too soon.

Overall, I'm moderately all right. So far. I don't feel angry or despairing, nor am I expecting to see Frank walk in the door. It's the small things that cause the pangs: the letters still addressed to him; the realisation that it is now 'I' rather than 'we'; that a widow is altogether different from a wife. I'm no longer one of a give-and-take partnership; I no longer have an unshakable point of reference.

I've been down to the churchyard more or less each day, and cannot hold back the tears. This morning the grave was dappled with sunlight, but the flowers are beginning to wilt. The plain cardboard marker says: FRANK CRAIG, and that, I'm afraid, is the stark reality.

A letter this morning encapsulates my state of mind exactly. 'I remember with a shudder', writes a widowed friend,

> the loneliness, the insecurity, the vulnerability of being left alone with responsibility and of no longer being the centre of someone else's life, and of having the focus of one's own life suddenly removed. I think it is the combination of the pain of loss and the dislocation of pattern in one's life that makes it all seem so bewildering and hopeless.

She refers to the return of suffering into my life. 'Does it feel more like the return of an old friend or an old enemy?' she asks. 'It is sometimes difficult to know the difference.' I am reminded of the Dalai Lama's teaching that 'My enemy is my friend' – meaning that it is only by learning to accept the enemy (be it person, thing or event) that one learns the practice of patience. The Sermon on the Mount, of course, preaches the same message about accepting the people who (or the things which) thwart or persecute us. Not exactly a popular idea today.

The bill for the funeral arrived, referring to Frank as 'the deceased' and 'the late Mr Craig'. Little pin-pricks, which mercilessly underline the fact that *he is dead*. Nick comes down to tell me that the former newscaster, Peter Woods, has died. He's just heard it on the six o'clock BBC News, to which he is an avid listener. 'So', he said, 'Dad's died, and now Peter Woods is dead.' He was quite matter-of-fact about it. Oh, to be Nick!

This evening, I reread the transcripts of the Bel Mooney BBC interviews on bereavement, *Perspectives for Living*.[39] In her introduction, she quotes Lily Pincus (who wrote *Death and the Family*) as saying that accepting the reality of loss is one of the major tasks of mourning; and that this crisis is 'probably the most severe crisis in human existence'. Bereavement, says Pincus, 'places you permanently on the interface between suffering and acceptance, bestowing the knowledge that death is simultaneously an individual outrage and something which is, after all, quite ordinary'.

Of all the interviews in the collection, I have always liked best the Christopher Booker one. I first read it just after Frank and I had visited Salisbury Cathedral and seen the magnificent Laurence Whistler windows commemorating the deaths of Booker's two sisters, Joanna and Serena. I bought two postcards of the engraved windows. Both show a rose radiating a light which penetrates and dispels the surrounding darkness. In one the light illuminates the Dorset countryside where the sisters had lived, and it carries one of my favourite quotations from 'Little Gidding', the one about 'the moment of the rose' and 'the moment of the yew tree' being of equal duration. It used to bring me great comfort, when Frank was dying, to reflect that life and death are interwoven, and that nothing and no one is ever lost.

The second engraving is similar, except that the light is even more powerful. Eliot, again:

> And all shall be well and
> All manner of thing shall be well
> When the tongues of flame are infolded
> Into the crowned knot of fire
> And the fire and the rose are one.[40]

For Booker, this 'wonderful meditation in glass' affirms the triumph of light over darkness:

> Laurence himself used the phrase. He said the light needs the darkness to become articulate. And that for me is the most important thing about living through tragedies so close to one: that actually through that darkness you do come to see. They give you the chance to find the light . . . All these experiences have immeasurably deepened my appreciation of this great polarity between death and life, and darkness and light, and how the true light is something eternal and shines forever out of these specific, awful, imprisoning experiences which leave one so confused. In the end the most important thing was to find meaning in them.[41]

He speaks of death as being absorbed into life itself – 'the love that moves the sun and other stars' – and disagrees with the famous Donne assertion that other people's deaths diminish us. On the contrary, our lives can be enhanced and enlarged by accepting the reality of death. 'It is absolutely in the centre of all our lives, both the deaths of others and our own eventual death.'

Thursday 23 March 1995

The letters continue to pour in, bringing a certain comfort. Not one of them is trite, they all seem to be written from the heart and so they help a great deal.

I ordered the memorial cards today, from the Carmelites at Wood Hall. In the end, after much deliberation, I chose the same prayer I had chosen for my mother, because it seems to sum up, very simply, what I believe about life: *Life is only for Love. Time is only that we may find God.*

Friday 24 March 1995

Small needle-pricks of pain: packets of Shredded Wheat; receiving his cancelled passport from the Passport Office; getting bills addressed to me only; getting bills and appeals addressed to us both; seeing his airline bag still hanging in the downstairs cloakroom; buying petrol; finding his foam cushion still in the boot of the car; seeing his terrible scrawled helpless entries on the last cheque-book stubs.

I am kept afloat by the loving support of friends and family. I was at Sue's for lunch; Nick's just come back from the day centre; Mark, Trish and the children are coming tonight for the week-end. But the void remains, rendering everything insubstantial. *'Un seul être vous manque et tout est dépeuplé.'* One person is lost to you and your entire world is empty. I didn't think it would be true for me, but that is the way it feels. The future does seem just an empty horizon.

Monday 27 March 1995

Yesterday was Mother's Day, and the whole family was here.

Timmy, aided by Mark in the background, brought me some breakfast – a bowl of muesli and a mug of tea – and refused to let me get out of bed until he'd done so. It was about 10 a.m. when it arrived, so, whether I wanted it or not, I had a lie-in! Later Trish gave me a framed montage which she'd made, using photos of Frank, the Valentine announcement in *The Times*, the card he'd sent with flowers on the day we moved in to this house – and the sprig of rosemary a friend had given me to wear at the funeral. I knew what it was as soon as I saw the large package, and the floodgates opened again. But although it made me unbearably sad, at the same time I was overwhelmed by the present, not least because of all the love and consideration that had gone into the making of it. I'm lucky in my daughter-in-law.

It was good to have the children around and in the afternoon Anthony unexpectedly arrived, on his way back to Gloucester after lunching with a friend. He came to check if there was any post that needed his immediate attention (he's looking after the business end of things) – and to bring me a Mother's Day card. Anthony is fairly undemonstrative and frequently forgets to sign his cards (though he never forgets to send one). Or he just signs them 'Anthony', with no greeting. But this time the card, signed 'For you and Dad, now and forever' carried a great emotional charge and I was very touched.

On getting up this morning, reaction to all yesterday's emotion set in. I felt flat and restless. I tried to trace the feeling to its source. It's partly grief; partly the disruption of life's familiar pattern; partly fear of being alone, fear of boredom, fear of being afraid. I haven't yet been faced with a serious crisis and fear that when one comes it will knock me for six.

Boredom at least is unlikely for the next few weeks. Work

has begun on the new conservatory on which Frank had set his heart. He had really looked forward to sitting in there in his wheelchair – he'd even made sure the door would be wheelchair-width – but fate decreed otherwise. In any case, listening to the racket downstairs, and seeing the chaos and confusion all around, I don't know how he'd have stood it. Perhaps it is just as well he didn't have to.

After Mass last Saturday evening, a parishioner, Monica Lee, told me she is going to embroider a kneeler for Douai Abbey in memory of Frank. What original ideas people have.

Tuesday 28 March 1995

Danielle's second birthday. She and the baby – now imminently expected – are going to have birthdays very close together. Fiona from the Julian group came to the door with a letter. She had been at the graveside for Frank's burial and felt the experience as very special. She writes:

> I had never met Frank – I had only come to know him through prayers and from sharing with others his journey as he was drawn towards God's fullness and glory. I felt he was a very special person – one who was much loved and gave much love. I found myself seemingly receiving something from him – or through him – as we stood together amidst such sadness, loss and grief – a great sense of peace, of hope and of wonderful love. It conveyed to me that Frank was very special, and for me he will remain so, as I remember that day with tenderness, fondness, awe and a great many thanks.

Upheld by such letters, as I am, I really cannot understand

those who request 'No, letters, please'. They are cutting themselves off from human warmth and kindness. I could not have survived – or survive now – without my friends.

Wednesday 29 March 1995

I said to Madeleine this morning that I'm all take and no give at present. She disagreed. 'You're giving the givers what *they* need,' she said. I understood what she meant: most people are glad of the opportunity to reach out to those in trouble. When Dekyi Tsering, the present Dalai Lama's mother, was dying, she worried about being a nuisance to everybody. Yet everyone I spoke to in the family claimed that it had been an exceptional joy and privilege to look after her. I know there are exceptions to the rule, but on the whole people do long to help. My friends are currently being presented with a human being adrift from her moorings, and they are taking it on themselves to make sure I don't drift too far downstream. For the present I can only gratefully accept their help. *The Stature of Waiting* again. The periods of enforced helplessness in our lives have greater spiritual potential than the times of frantic 'achieving'.

I have a sudden memory of a woman pharmacist in Cracow during the dreadful days that followed the introduction of martial law in Poland. I had travelled to Warsaw and Cracow as escort to a van load of medical supplies sent by Medical Aid for Poland (and I was at the same time slipping away to meet Lech Walesa and other Solidarity leaders about whom I was writing a book) and this emergency pharmacy was one of the few sources of supply for the suffering Poles. They queued from first light, in drenching rain or driving snow, in hopes of finding the items written on their prescription, which was otherwise a worthless piece of paper. 'Do you know what my dream is?' the pharmacist asked me, as I watched her stack away the treasured drugs after checking them. 'It's that one day I'll be in a position to give to other people in need, rather than always being at the receiving end.' I knew exactly what she meant, and sympathised, but there was a greatness about her and so many others like her.

Thursday 30 March 1995

The periods of helplessness eventually pass. Unless we let ourselves cling to the what-might-have-been-if-only with bitterness and resentment in our hearts, life must return. Right now any activity I undertake is merely a way of passing the time; but I must be patient and wait for the moment when I can be involved in life again. The process cannot, unfortunately, be rushed.

Wednesday 5 April 1995

I understand the temptation to turn one's back on reality, to run away, turn to drink, drugs, self-pity or whatever. It would be easy to despair at this low point. I was buoyed up by family visitors all week-end. When they went, I wept. Then Shirley came this morning and took me out to a splendid lunch and I felt much better. But after she'd gone, the gloom descended again. Black dog on my shoulder. I'm going to have to get used to this. In the end no one can really get me out of the trough but me.

On Friday afternoon the house was broken into, and in my weak-kneed state the shock has absolutely pulverised me. I was out for only two hours, Nicole Bentham having asked me to lunch with her and John. When I came back, the front door was chained from the inside and, getting in via the back door, I found the kitchen window swinging open. At the top of the stairs I could see an upturned drawer which had contained – mainly cheap and cheerful ethnic – jewellery. I rang the police and asked Anthony if he'd come and spend the week-end here. Anne and Mike came straight over and arranged for a security firm to come and fit more locks, etc. Now it feels like Fort Knox and I'm miserable – as if I've lost all pleasure in the house. I feel menaced somehow. Needless to say, at this crisis I miss Frank more than ever and am very weepy. It isn't that I had anything of great value (whoever it was must have discovered that to his chagrin) but – as everyone always reports when they've been burgled – it's the fact that someone got in the house, went through the rooms, tipped out drawers, invaded one's privacy that is so distressing. Suddenly I am again terribly insecure, unwilling to leave the house, because of the fear of coming back again.

Today, the loneliness and misery are so acute, it's almost as if I didn't know what the pain of separation was until now. I can't stop crying. I long for Frank to come in and put his arms round me and calm my fears. Why did he have to leave me? Yes, yes, I know why. But still, why? We can't always be rational about things. Or even philosophical. I feel I can't go on.

The worst did eventually pass, but I still feel shaky. Let's look on the bright side: a lot of good things have happened too. It would have been Frank's birthday on Tuesday, and Anthony insisted on my getting away from the house. Talking to my friend, Anna Benjamin, at Frank's funeral, he had discovered that Christopher (her husband who is in the RSC) was currently doing a season at Stratford. Anthony had promptly booked two tickets for *Romeo and Juliet*. I was still too hung over to enjoy the play properly, but Christopher was outstanding as Old Capulet and it was good to be with old friends. Next morning we went for a long walk by the river Avon with Anna, took her out to lunch and came back home. I dreaded coming into the house, but everything was as I had left it.

Good news came almost immediately, as Mark rang to say that a baby girl had been born earlier that day – that is, on Frank's birthday. We are all delighted. As she is ten days overdue, we feel she must have waited to be born on 11 April. Frank had hoped from the first that 'it' would be born on his birthday, though of course he didn't know then that he would no longer be with us. Still, a little bit of him has come back into the world with this new grandchild, who is to be called Rebecca Frances (the Frances being in his honour). Life goes on regardless.

I've now made a kind of resolution to begin each day with thanks for the many and various good things in my life: my family and friends; interesting work if and when I can find the energy to get back to it; reasonable health; comfortable house. I strive to believe, really deep-down believe, that God is present and active in all this darkness. Like Bonhoeffer, I want to be 'so sure of God's guiding hand that I hope I shall be kept in that certainty'. In prison, and shortly before his execution by the Nazis at Flossenburg Concentration Camp, Bonhoeffer wrote: 'I am firmly convinced – however strange it may seem – that my life has followed a straight and unbroken course. It has been an uninterrupted enrichment of experience, for which I can only be thankful.' And again: 'What is happiness and unhappiness? It depends so little on the circumstances. It depends really on that which happens inside a person.'[42]

I wrote something similar in *Blessings*, and have always cherished the moment in that little book *Song for Sarah*, when the author, Paula d'Arcy, realises that she is done with the self-pity which has consumed her since the death of her husband and daughter in a car-crash. Since her situation is not going to change, it is she who must do so. 'It will not change, so *I* must.' Change must be embraced; a new self must emerge from the wreckage of the old. 'Life glitters between the two darknesses of birth and death,' says another bereaved writer.[43] We are changed by these traumatic events in our lives. The world never looks quite the same again; we are not quite as at home in it as we were before. But within those new parameters, we set off on a new path and begin to live again. In this week's *Tablet*, Lionel Blue writes of the moment when he realised that 'Prayer would not change the world for me, only give me the courage to face it.' That is such a valuable lesson to learn, but always difficult. It means accepting the new pattern in life's ever-shifting kaleidoscope.

A Quaker friend of Frank's, Marilyn, sends me some words of William Penn, written in 1693. They seem very suited to this Easter season. I found one passage in particular very moving: 'And this is the comfort of the good, that the grave cannot hold them and that they live as soon as they die. For death is no more than a turning of us over from time to eternity. Since Death, then, is the way and condition of life, we cannot love to live if we cannot bear to die.'[44]

Holy Saturday, 15 April 1995

I've begun listening avidly to *Thought for the Day* on Radio 4, hoping for crumbs of comfort. For the last few Saturdays, it's been David Winter, but today Eric James spoke on the loss and desolation which followed the first Good Friday, when all seemed lost, with nothing to hope for. But, he said, we must believe that God will turn everything to good, and he quoted some lines from Edith Sitwell:

> Love is not changed by death
> Nothing is lost
> And all in the end is harvest.[45]

But the harvest depends on *me*. And I'm not yet ready for it.

Still, there's so much to be happy about. I'm being showered with affection. Mark came over for twenty-four hours; Anthony arrived for the week-end; Frances came for a few days last week; Elzbieta rang, André and Françoise, Frank Longford. Flowers came from Margaret and John and from the people who bought our other house; and in the evening Vincent came with a bouquet from him and Barbara. It is nearly Easter, when the message is all of hope.

Easter Sunday, 16 April 1995

I went to the 8 a.m. Mass which these days I find more appealing than the long Easter Vigil. Less dramatic, but more prayerful. 'I hope the Easter message gets through to you, Mary,' Roger Royle said on the phone yesterday. 'It's terribly important that it should. You need it more than ever now.' So what I have to take on board is that light always conquers darkness, life ultimately overcomes death. All shall be well, and all shall be well . . . I believe it to be true, but it is too early yet for my heart to respond. One day it will, but the healing can't be rushed. The grieving has to be gone through to the end.

I must make a start, though, by overcoming my deep reluctance to go anywhere, do anything. I told Mark about my determination to begin each day with a thank you. He said, 'Yes, with a thank you, but also with a plan, however small. What you need now is to rouse yourself out of a negative approach to life.' There's a preview of paintings by local artists in Woolton Hill today. I will go to it.

There's comfort in the prayer Tim Horsington, Rector of the Highclere parish, brought for me:

> Lord, I know that life can never be the same again. The one I loved has been taken from me, and I am conscious of an acute loneliness, an inner emptiness; and life seems to have lost its meaning. Yet, I know, Lord, that I am not alone, for you are with me, and I know that my loved one is not dead or lost but is alive and safe in your keeping. And I know that death is not the end, and that life is still full of meaning, for your promises cannot fail and your love is unchanging. Lord, I know all these things. I ask you to make them real to me. Above all, I ask you to make yourself real to me at this time, as my trusted Master and Friend; for while life may never be the same again, you are always the same, yesterday, and today, and forever. Amen.

I shall try and return to writing soon. It will be hard at first, but it can be done. I shall think about returning to Dharamsala and picking up the threads of the book about the Dalai Lama and his family. And I shall give more time to my friends, who are so determined to pull me through. I flick back the pages of this journal and see that I have written on the inside cover an extract from Joyce Grenfell's 'If I should go before the rest of you':

> Weep if you must,
> Parting is hell,
> But life goes on,
> So sing as well.[46]

I am still insecure, still vulnerable, still liable to be knocked off course by the least little contrary wind. But I know that in time all this will pass. And, though there may indeed come further troubles which are beyond my capacity to overcome, nevertheless, as Margaret Spufford wrote in her inspiring book about suffering, 'by some persisting miracle of grace, the memories of the past and the pain of the present, do prove capable of healing or at least of transformation. I cannot comprehend the process, but I am sometimes overwhelmed by wonder at it and thanksgiving for it.'[47]

Life, with all its tragic flaws, is still a rare and wonderful gift. It has much to teach us, and we have much to give back. Life and death are two halves of the same whole. Lent is over, Easter is here.

> Water gushes in the desert,
> streams in the wasteland,
> the scorched earth becomes a lake,
> the parched land springs of water
>
> > (Isaiah 35:7)

Or, as Auden put it more recently,

> In the deserts of the heart
> Let the healing fountain start.[48]

My heart *is* a desert right now, but the healing fountain is somewhere hidden in its wastes. One day there will be a resurrection. I am absolutely certain of it.

Notes

1. Donald Nicholl, *Holiness*, Darton, Longman and Todd, 1981.
2. *God of the Impossible: Daily Readings with Carlo Carretto*, ed. Robin Baird-Smith, Darton, Longman and Todd.
3. Sheila Cassidy, *Good Friday People*, Darton, Longman and Todd. See also her *Sharing the Darkness* and *The Loneliest Journey*.
4. Teilhard de Chardin, *Le Milieu Divin: An Essay on the Interior Life*, Fontana, 1964.
5. Erich Fromm, *To Have or To Be?*, Abacus, 1979.
6. Viktor E. Frankl, *Man's Search for Meaning: An Introduction to Logotherapy*, Hodder and Stoughton, 1964.
7. Sogyal Rinpoche, *The Tibetan Book of Living and Dying*, Random House, 1992.
8. *God of the Impossible*.
9. Hermann Hesse, *Siddhartha*, Bantam.
10. Quoted by Brigid Marlin in her anthology, *From East to West: Awakening to a Spiritual Search*, Fount, 1989; Chögyam Trunggpa, *Cutting through Spiritual Materialism*, Shambala, 1973.
11. Francis Thompson, 'The Kingdom of God'.
12. R. S. Thomas, 'Via Negativa', *Later Poems 1972–1982*, Papermac.
13. *The Upanishads: Breath of the Eternal*, Vedanta Press, 1983.
14. *Bhagavad Gita: The Song of God*, Dent, 1975.
15. *Tao Te Ching*, Penguin, 1963.
16. *Universal Wisdom: A Journey through the Sacred Wisdom of the World*, ed. Bede Griffiths, Fount, 1994.
17. Hesse, *Siddhartha*.
18. W. H. Vanstone, *Love's Endeavour, Love's Expense: The Response of Being to the Love of God*, Darton, Longman and Todd, 1977.
19. Shantideva, *A Guide to the Bodhisattva's Way of Life*, Tibetan Library, Dharamsala, 1979.
20. W. H. Vanstone, *The Stature of Waiting*, Darton, Longman and Todd, 1982.
21. Frederick Franck, Introduction to *The World of Angelus Silesius*, Wildwood.
22. Dag Hammarskjøld, *Markings*, Faber and Faber, 1964.
23. Teilhard de Chardin, *Le Milieu Divin*, Fontana, 1967.
24. Michael Hollings and Etta Gullick, *The One Who Listens*, Mayhew McCrimmon, 1971.
25. Elie Wiesel, *Night*, translated from the French by Stella Rodway, Fontana, 1960.
26. William Styron, *Sophie's Choice*, Jonathan Cape, 1976.
27. Hammarskjøld, *Markings*.

28. *Selected Poems of Rainer Maria Rilke*, ed. Robert Bly, Harper, 1981.
29. T. S. Eliot, *The Four Quartets*, Faber and Faber, 1948.
30. Philip Toynbee, *Part of a Journey: An Autobiographical Journal, 1977–79*, Collins, 1981.
31. George Herbert, 'The Temper', *The Metaphysical Poets*, Penguin.
32. Mary O'Hara, *Celebration of Love*, Hodder and Stoughton, 1985.
33. 'That Nature is a Heraclitean Fire', *Selection of Poems and Prose of Gerard Manley Hopkins*, Penguin, 1953.
34. William Shakespeare, *Cymbeline*.
35. From the Penguin translation of the *Upanishads*. I discovered this translation later and preferred it to the one I had originally written here.
36. To my intense grief, Mary Tuck, an eminent social researcher and criminologist, died suddenly in October 1996, just as this book was going to the publishers.
37. *Enfolded in Love: Daily Readings with Julian of Norwich*, Darton, Longman and Todd, 1980.
38. Alan Bennett, *Writing Home*, Faber and Faber, 1994.
39. Bel Mooney, *Perspectives for Living: Conversations on Bereavement and Love*, BBC, 1992.
40. Eliot, *The Four Quartets*.
41. Mooney, *Perspectives for Living*.
42. Dietrich Bonhoeffer, *Letters and Papers from Prison*, SCM Press, 1971.
43. Christopher Leach, *Letter to a Younger Son*, Arrow, 1981.
44. From Section 22.95, *Quaker Faith and Practice*, 1995.
45. Edith Sitwell, quoted on the radio.
46. Quoted by Mary O'Hara in *Celebration of Love*.
47. Margaret Spufford, *Celebration*, Fount, 1989.
48. W. H. Auden, 'In Memory of W. B. Yeats', *The Faber Book of Modern Verse*, Faber and Faber, 1965.